BASEBALL'S MOST
VALUABLE PLAYERS

BASEBALL'S MOST VALUABLE PLAYERS

by George Vecsey

illustrated with photographs

RANDOM HOUSE · NEW YORK

Library of Congress Catalog Card Number: 66-10692

Manufactured in the United States of America

Designed by Jackie Corner

CONTENTS

BASEBALL'S MOST VALUABLE PLAYERS

1
ABOUT THE
AWARD

The man who receives the Most Valuable Player award is set apart from other ballplayers. The award recognizes that he made a greater contribution to the success of his team during the previous season than any other player in his league. He is more than just an outstanding player; he is a good teammate, too. Almost every year the Most Valuable Player is baseball's biggest hero.

The players have great respect for the award. All season long they discuss who should receive it. Winning the MVP award is a highlight in any player's career. "I believe that many players would rather win the Most Valuable Player award than the batting championship," says one former star. "There's something about it that says 'You're the best' and players regard it as the highest compliment that can be paid them."

Each fall two baseball reporters from each major-league city elect the Most Valuable Player in each major league. They are members of the Baseball Writers' Association and most of them take the award very seriously, often debating among themselves about who deserves it most.

The Baseball Writers' Association first gave the award in 1931. There had been other MVP awards in earlier years, but the writers' award was soon recognized as the most authoritative. The award could

3

have been given to the "most outstanding" player.
But the writers recognized that an "outstanding"
player is not always the most valuable. They wanted
to reward both ability and team play. The award
was to go to the man who did the most for his team
in one season. He did not have to be the most
talented man in baseball.

Some seasons it is easy to pick a winner. One man
stands out in his league. Perhaps he drives in 110
runs or wins 20 games, and his team wins the pennant. Then the voting is easy. But many times it is
more difficult. Do you pick a .275 hitter who sparked
his team to a pennant or a .350 hitter who slugged
his team into second place? Do you pick a pitcher
who won twenty-five games for a third-place team
or one who won eighteen games for the pennant-
winners?

In 1964, for instance, the New York Mets obtained
veteran shortstop Roy McMillan from Milwaukee.
The day he arrived, Met opponents stopped making
singles on easy ground balls. The Mets started to
make double plays. And, although he was only a
.214 hitter, McMillan won many games with his
bunting and his ability to hit-and-run. Even more
important, McMillan helped the other Met infielders.
They gained a great deal from his skill, experience and
generosity. But the Mets still finished tenth.

In the same year the St. Louis Cardinals won the pennant. They had many outstanding ballplayers. But Ken Boyer, the strapping third baseman, had driven in 119 runs and been the quiet leader of his team. Roy McMillan may have been every bit as valuable to the Mets as Ken Boyer was to the Cardinals—but the Cardinals won the pennant and Boyer got the award.

Understandably the emphasis is on winners. Of the first 70 awards, 49 of them went to players on pennant-winning teams. Only three times did a player on a second division team win it. Chicago Cubs slugger Hank Sauer won in 1952 and Cub star Ernie Banks in 1958 and 1959, although the Cubs finished in fifth place each year.

Although rookies are eligible for the award, no rookie has ever won it. Most Valuable Players are judged partly on experience and leadership. And even if a rookie is a great player, he has not usually had time to become a team leader. The winners are usually thoroughly experienced players.

Only twelve pitchers have been included among the first seventy winners. The writers have felt that a pitcher doesn't usually contribute as much as a regular player because he works only one day out of four. As a result a special citation for pitchers, the Cy Young award, was instituted in 1956.

Many great players have never won the award. Babe Ruth, Ty Cobb, Cy Young and Walter Johnson played before it was established in 1931. Others, such as Mel Ott, Ralph Kiner, Bob Feller and Warren Spahn, were never MVPs because they had their best years when another player was having an even better one.

Many kinds of players have been named Most Valuable Player. Some were not great but could inspire their teams to great performances. Scrappy players like Frankie Frisch and Jackie Robinson used determination and competitive spirit as well as their skills to win many pennants. Others, like Yogi Berra and Stan Musial, were not inspirational in the same way but were great clutch ballplayers and provided a quiet example for their teams.

There was even an occasional star like Ted Williams, who was unpopular with some reporters and fans, but whose magnificent hitting kept the Boston Red Sox in contention for many years. Williams would never have won a popularity contest—but he was voted Most Valuable Player twice.

Many of the Most Valuable Players are in Baseball's Hall of Fame or will be voted into the Hall after they have retired. Others may have had one or more great years and contributed greatly to their teams. But their accomplishments are not quite enduring enough to merit election into the Hall.

The Most Valuable Player may be great or merely good. He may be an inspirational leader, an abrasive hard-driving player or a quiet example. The important thing is that he benefit his team and lead it to heights that would have been impossible without him. His value depends not only upon his personal success but also on the success of his team. This book has been written to show how some of the greatest MVPs combined personal and team achievement to win the coveted award.

2
WILLIE MAYS

Most Valuable Player, National League, 1954, 1965

Willie Mays had the energy of a boy in 1951. The rookie center fielder of the New York Giants was only twenty years old. Every day during the season he couldn't wait to get dressed so that he could play catch before the game. Giant manager Leo Durocher ofter played "pepper" with his star just to keep him busy. Durocher would slap grounders at Mays, hitting them harder and harder and farther and farther away. Willie would chase them and dive for them, laughing and chattering in his squeaky voice. He never seemed to tire.

When Willie had free time in New York, he even played stickball in the streets. He lived in Harlem, near the Polo Grounds, the Giants' home park. One of his many young friends would throw a rubber ball and Willie would swing a broomstick.

"It's good for my batting eye," he said. "If you can hit that little ball with that little stick, you can sure hit a baseball with a big bat."

One day a policeman caught Willie and his friends playing stickball in the street. He scolded them and told them to find a safer place to play. Later he learned that the older man in the pack was Willie Mays, the new center fielder for the Giants.

Willie had been playing ball since he was a boy in Alabama. The Giants had spotted him when he was playing in a Negro league, where he was the youngest player. He signed with the Giants and the next season he batted .477 at Minneapolis, the Giants' highest farm team. The Giants brought him up to the majors in May, 1951. At first Willie didn't hit much, but he soon established himself in other ways. In July he made a defensive play against the Brooklyn Dodgers that made him the talk of the baseball world.

It happened in the eighth inning of a tie game.

Willie makes one of the catches that made him a sensation even before he became a great hitter.

The Dodgers had runners on first and third with one out. The batter, Carl Furillo, smashed a line drive to deep right center field. Mays had to run hard for the ball. Moving directly away from the plate, he stuck out his glove and just managed to make the catch. But since he was still moving toward the outfield fence, it seemed almost certain that the runner on third would tag up and score.

Somehow Mays managed to pivot to his left foot as soon as he caught the ball. With a violent turn he heaved the ball toward home plate—without even looking toward the infield. The ball traveled 450 feet on the fly, landing in the catcher's mitt. The runner was out by five feet. That ended the inning and the Giants went on to win the game, 3–1. Players and fans all over the country talked about the play for months.

By September they were talking about the Giants. The Dodgers had led the Giants by 13½ games in mid-August. But the Giants went on a winning streak and caught the Dodgers in the final days of the season, forcing a play-off series. The Dodgers and Giants each won one game. Then, with the Dodgers ahead in the final game, Bobby Thomson hit a dramatic ninth-inning home run to win the pennant for the Giants. Willie was chosen Rookie of the Year.

The next year, 1952, Willie was called into the Army after playing 36 games. The New York fans were sad to see him go and even the umpires waved good-bye to him after his last game. But the Giants missed him more than anyone. They lost three straight games and fell out of first place as soon as he left. They finished second in 1952 and fell all the way to fifth place in 1953.

Mays returned to the Giants at the start of the 1954 season. Soon the team began laughing again—and started winning, too. Willie's teammates slapped towels at him in the locker room. They squirted shaving cream at him when he was in the shower. They wrestled with him and teased him. When he hit a home run or made an exciting catch, they gave him the silent treatment. Then Willie would burst into laughter and his teammates would laugh, too. It was a happy year.

Willie was twenty-three years old in 1954 but he still had the energy of a boy. He led the league in batting with a .345 average, hit 41 homers and drove in 110 runs. He became a daring base runner and continued to make remarkable catches in center field. The Giants ran away with the pennant and they won four straight games from Cleveland in the World Series. There was no doubt that Willie had revived the Giants after his two years in the Army. In November he was voted Most Valuable Player, becoming one of the youngest men ever to receive the award.

After the 1957 season the Giants left the Polo Grounds and moved across the country to San Francisco. San Francisco's hills and bridges, cable cars and ocean liners, Chinatown and Fisherman's Wharf make it a lovely city. Visitors often think it is the most attractive city in the United States. In 1958 San Francisco had a new attraction to match the Golden Gate Bridge—Willie Mays.

Almost down on one knee, Willie smacks out another hit.

Willie was as good as ever. The San Francisco fans soon learned to appreciate his basket catches, with his glove held at his waist. They came to anticipate his cap flying off whenever he roared around the bases. They learned to cheer when he tapped his glove. They knew it was a sign that he would catch the ball.

The Giants won their first pennant for San Francisco in 1962, beating the Dodgers in another play-off. Willie drove in 141 runs that season, more than in any previous season. But Maury Wills of the Dodgers, who stole 104 bases that season, edged him out as Most Valuable Player.

Meanwhile, Willie was growing older. He turned thirty-one in 1962. The boy who had helped win pennants in 1951 and 1954 was now a grown man with a son of his own. He didn't laugh as much as he had when he was twenty-three, and he was no longer the center of locker-room horseplay. He had bought a home and he worked for a bank in the winter. He no longer had time to play stickball in the streets.

The regular baseball season took all his energy now. In 1962 he fainted in the Giant dugout during a game and was unconscious for ten minutes. Doctors said he was overtired and made him rest in the hospital for a few days. But he came back to help win the pennant.

In 1963 Willie collapsed while he was at bat with the bases loaded in the first inning of a tense Labor Day double-header. Fans gasped as he sank to his knees and crawled in a circle around home plate. Once again doctors sent him home to rest.

After the Giants finished in fourth place in 1964,

they appointed a new manager, Herman Franks, for the 1965 season. Franks had been an assistant to Manager Leo Durocher when Mays joined the Giants in 1951. In fact Franks' big job in 1951 was to encourage Willie and help him get used to the major leagues. Willie liked Franks almost as much as he had liked Durocher.

Franks sometimes tried to play the fool. He would spit tobacco juice and pretend he didn't even know the time of day. But nobody was fooled. He had been a successful businessman and he knew how to manage a baseball team, too. He also had a way of making Mays feel happy. In 1965 Willie Mays became Most Valuable Player again.

Willie's 1965 season was a textbook example on "How to Be a Most Valuable Player." He did everything but pilot the team plane. He hit 29 homers in the last two months of the season, although he was often exhausted. He finished with 52 homers for the season, the most in his career, and batted .317. He missed only five games.

But his value went beyond statistics. Willie had been named captain in 1962. By 1965 he was helping nearly everybody on his team. His locker was right at the crossroads of the clubhouse and the players passed him on their way to the showers, the field, the manager's office and the parking lot. Nearly everyone stopped to talk with him. One day, in a conversation with Hal Lanier, Willie advised the young second baseman to take charge of the infield. Soon Lanier was calling for more than his share of pop flies and was giving encouragement to all the Giant pitchers. Lanier was becoming a leader on the field because Willie had encouraged him.

One of Willie's official duties as captain was to bring the Giant line-up card to the umpire at the start of the game. But by 1965 he was even helping to prepare it. Willie and the coaches held a conference with manager Franks before every game. Willie listened to the coaches, but made suggestions of his own, too.

In one game Manager Franks wanted to rest Willie. He had gone hitless over the weekend and the last-place Mets were in town. It seemed a good time for him to sit out a game.

But Willie approached Franks at the batting cage before the game. "Hey, Skip," Willie said, "Mousie has a bad cold. I'm going to play center and you can play Gabe in left and Kenny in right."

Willie was telling the manager that Matty Alou (Mousie) had a cold. Len Gabrielson would stay in left field, Ken Henderson would play right field and Willie would replace Alou in center.

"What's the matter with Mousie?" Franks asked suspiciously.

"Cold," Mays repeated. "He's on the trainer's table. He doesn't feel too good."

"You sure?" Franks persisted.

"Sure," Mays said.

"This is the fifteenth time I've changed my line-up card today," Franks blustered. "But if you say so . . ." And the manager scribbled Mays' name into the line-up in place of Alou.

On the day he was supposed to rest, Willie won the game. He smashed a home run for the first run of the day. Later he walked, raced to third on a single and scored on a short fly ball. The Giants won the game, 3–2.

In August Willie won an important game in Houston's Astrodome. The Giants had won eleven straight games and were closing in on the Dodgers. But this night the Astros were ahead, 5–3, with two outs in the ninth inning. There was a Giant runner on base and Willie Mays was up. The crowd sat up in their seats, hoping that the Astros could last for one more out.

There wasn't much doubt that Mays would be "going for downtown," trying for a home run. Houston pitcher Claude Raymond threw five straight fastballs —three balls and two strikes. Then Mays fouled off four more fastballs. Twice he swung so hard he spun to his knees. Then Raymond came in with his tenth fastball. This one went downtown—it was a tremendous drive into the center-field stands and it tied the game. The Giants won in extra innings.

The highlight of Willie's season came later in August against the Los Angeles Dodgers. Willie had always played his best against the Dodgers, ever since the Giants and Dodgers had both played in New York. First place was at stake in this four-game series. Mays was tired but the huge crowds at Candlestick Park made him forget his exhaustion.

In the first game he hit a two-run homer. In the second game he hit a two-run homer. In the third game he hit a one-run homer. But the Dodgers won two of the three games.

The fourth game was one of Mays' finest. The Giants were tense: they needed a victory to stay in the pennant race. The game was played under gray skies, and a chilly wind whipped through the stadium. The capacity crowd of 42,807 shivered under blankets as Juan Marichal of the Giants opposed the Dodgers' Sandy Koufax.

The Dodgers had a 2–1 lead on Marichal, who was struggling hard on the mound. When Marichal came to bat in the third, nobody was prepared for what happened. Suddenly he turned around and started to smash John Roseboro, the Dodger catcher, over the head with the bat.

Both teams dashed to home plate and tried to separate the two men. But Marichal kept trying to get at the Dodger catcher. Roseboro fell sideways. Now other players grew angry. Another Giant raised his bat. Dodger players began to raise their fists. Roseboro, with blood pouring down his face, kept struggling to reach Marichal. Marichal, restrained by Giant coaches, shouted and gestured at Roseboro. If Roseboro had gotten loose, a full-scale brawl could have ensued. Then Willie Mays entered the scene.

Willie raced to home plate. He saw Roseboro, a good friend of his during the winter, bleeding from the head. Willie feared that the blood was streaming from Roseboro's eye.

"Johnny, Johnny, you're hurt, you're hurt bad," Mays said. This made Roseboro stop struggling. Mays persuaded him to go to the clubhouse for help. The umpires and police restored order on the field and the other players, seeing Mays comfort a Dodger, stopped fighting. Marichal was banished from the game.

Before Roseboro left, Mays saw that his friend was bleeding from a scalp wound, not from his eye. "You'll be all right," Mays said. He visited Roseboro in the Dodger clubhouse while the Giants were at bat, instead of sitting in the Giant dugout. That evening, when Roseboro left town with the rest of the Dodgers, he wore a cap over the bandage on his scalp. It was a San Francisco Giant cap—belonging to Willie Mays.

The Dodgers were angry with Marichal and other Giants, but they had high praise for Mays. "Without Willie Mays, there would have been a lot more fighting," Dodger outfielder Lou Johnson said.

The game had continued after Marichal was sent to the showers. Bob Schroder, the pinch hitter, struck out. Tito Fuentes flied out. Then Koufax suddenly grew wild. He walked Jim Davenport and Willie McCovey on eight straight pitches. That brought up Mays.

"I knew Koufax was shook up," Mays said. "After that incident, Sandy didn't have his real stuff."

Willie didn't give Koufax a chance to find his real stuff. He swung at the first pitch and laced it into the left-field stands for a three-run homer. The crowd stood and cheered for its hero, who had turned the game completely around. Koufax didn't allow any more runs but the Giants held onto a 4–3 victory.

For all his heroics, Willie couldn't quite win the pennant for the Giants. The Dodgers pulled away in the last ten days of the season, to finish two games ahead of the Giants. But in November, Willie Mays was voted Most Valuable Player again. Eleven years had passed since he first won the award.

"I felt I made more of a contribution to the team

Willie comforts Dodger catcher John Roseboro after Roseboro was attacked by Juan Marichal. Directly above Mays are Dodger manager Walt Alston and Sandy Koufax.

Mays slams his 512th homer early in the 1966 season. The blow made Mays the greatest home-run hitter in National League history.

this year than in 1954," he said. "That's because I was young then. Leo Durocher was the manager and he did most of the talking. I'm a veteran now. I can help the other players."

He was no longer the boy who played stickball in the streets. In addition to being one of the most talented players in the game, Willie had become an experienced veteran, the captain and leader of his team. He had become more valuable than ever.

3
FRANK FRISCH

Most Valuable Player, National League, 1931

In 1931 the baseball writers picked the Most Valuable Player in each league for the first time. Since most of the writers felt that the Most Valuable Player should come from the pennant-winning team, they were looking for a winner.

In the American League the Philadelphia Athletics ran away with the pennant. Athletics pitcher Lefty Grove won thirty-one games and lost only four. Grove was the natural choice and he became the first Most Valuable Player in the American League.

The National League winner was easy to pick, too. Frankie Frisch of the St. Louis Cardinals had played thirteen seasons in the major leagues and, in 1931, he had played on his seventh pennant-winning team.

Frisch had been groomed to be a most valuable player from the day he put on his major-league uniform. His first manager would not have tolerated any other kind of player. Frisch joined the New York Giants in 1919. The Giant manager was John J. McGraw, the toughest manager in baseball. McGraw had gained his toughness playing for the Baltimore Orioles, a rugged team that had won several major league races in the 1890s. The Orioles couldn't afford injuries: if a man was hurt, he played anyhow and won. No excuses and no complaints were allowed. McGraw carried this spirit to the Giants.

McGraw was particularly suspicious of players who had gone to college. College men with fancy words and fancy manners were not for him. Frisch had come to the Giants straight from Fordham University, so McGraw was watching carefully when he put young Frisch into his first major league game.

The Giants were playing the first-place Cincinnati Reds late in the 1919 season. Frisch had been a short-stop at Fordham, but McGraw started him at third base. The first batter slammed a hard ground ball to third. Frankie was ready for it but the ball took a wicked bounce and crashed off his chest. He didn't waste time feeling for bruises. He dove for the ball and threw the runner out.

"I like that," McGraw said with a chuckle. "If he had made the play cleanly, I'd have paid no attention to it. But for a kid just breaking in and doing it before a crowd like that, to get a ball away from him—well, he's got guts."

From that day on there was room for Frisch on the New York Giants. He was McGraw's type despite his college education. It took Frisch two years to get used to major league pitching. But in 1921 he slashed a .341 average and became the Giants' most important player.

Frisch was a switch hitter. He was not too powerful but he hit line drives. He stole bases and drove in runs. Eventually he was moved to second base, where he still sometimes used his chest instead of his glove to stop ground balls. He got the job done, however.

Frisch led the Giants to four straight pennants from 1921 to 1924. If there had been a writers' Most Valuable Player award then, he might have won it every time. His averages during those four years were .341, .327, .348 and .328. He hit even better in the World Series.

McGraw soon appointed Frisch captain of the Giants. It was an honor—but also a burden. Although

Frank Frisch, the "Fordham Flash," warms up before a 1923 game when he was playing for McGraw's Giants.

McGraw was a skillful manager, he could be a vicious man. He would give a severe tongue-lashing to any player, but he saved the most vicious attacks for his captain.

The players understood this. When McGraw raved at the captain, he was really raving at all of them. If McGraw called Frisch an "ironhead" or something much worse, the players knew they were all "iron-heads." Baseball was not as gentle in the 1920s as it is now. Tempers and manners were worse. Many of the players were not even high-school graduates. They were country boys, used to harsh words and actions, and they accepted McGraw's harangues as normal.

But McGraw went too far in 1926. He was not a happy man that year and he picked on Frisch at the wrong time. Frankie was playing with sore legs, and he was playing badly. But he would not tell anybody about his troubles. He just kept playing, in the best McGraw fashion.

One night in Cincinnati Frisch missed a ground ball. McGraw chewed him out in the clubhouse. Frisch held his temper. He dressed quickly and left after the game but he could not forget the scolding.

The Giants traveled from Cincinnati to St. Louis. Frisch's legs were still aching as he went out to play the first game. A Cardinal runner reached first base and Frisch was assigned to cover second base if the runner attempted to steal. The runner broke for second with the pitch and Frisch rushed over to take the throw. But the batter slapped a ground ball right through the spot Frisch had vacated. It went for a hit-and-run single, moving the runner to third. "I couldn't have stopped the ball if I'd had a net on a long pole," Frisch said later.

Instead of giving credit to the batter, McGraw

snarled at Frisch. In front of the other players, he accused him of intentionally missing the ball. Frankie was hurt by McGraw's accusation and brooded about it all that night. In the morning he packed his suitcase and caught the noon train to New York. He didn't rejoin the Giants for two weeks. Everybody expected that Frisch would be traded after the season.

Frisch was traded—to the St. Louis Cardinals, the up-and-coming team in the National League. The Cardinal general manager, Branch Rickey, was building a powerhouse in St. Louis. Frisch was glad to be with the Cardinals, who were more relaxed than the Giants.

Though there was no hard-bitten manager to contend with, Frisch retained his old Oriole spirit and soon became the toughest Cardinal on the field. McGraw had been a good teacher.

Frankie didn't fight often. But his toughness was calculated to help the team. If an opponent was causing the Cardinals trouble, Frisch would take him on.

One year the Cardinals decided to do something about Boston's Burleigh Grimes, a spitball pitcher with a bad temper. Grimes had been firing beanballs at the Cardinals for years, and Frisch's head had been the prime target. Frankie volunteered to handle Grimes.

Frisch bunted down the first baseline, planning to collide with Grimes when he came over to field the ball. The strategy worked perfectly. When Grimes lumbered off the mound to field the ball, Frisch swerved right at him. But instead of colliding with him, Frisch stepped on his foot. His spikes caught Grimes in the ankle and the Boston pitcher was out of action for almost a month.

After Grimes had recovered, the two teams met again. Frisch sought out Grimes before the game, apparently thinking that an apology would save him from a bad beaning during the game. Frisch should have known better. The first pitch from Grimes sailed right at Frisch's head. Only a quick acrobatic dive saved Frankie from a serious injury.

Grimes watched with his hands on his hips as Frisch got up. "You didn't smile when you apologized," he shouted.

Anyone that tough seemed to belong with the Cardinals. They bought Grimes in 1930 and assigned him to room with Frisch. The two hardheads shook hands and became friends. But they never doubted what would happen if they ever became opponents again.

One hot afternoon in St. Louis in 1931, Grimes gave up a homer to Philadelphia's Chuck Klein in the first inning. The score was still 1–0 after the first half of the ninth. When the Cardinals made two outs in the last half of the inning, Grimes left the dugout. Angry with the Cardinal hitters, he stomped into the clubhouse and began tearing off his uniform—without bothering to unbutton the buttons.

By the time he had finished tearing off his uniform, Grimes heard his teammates roaring into the clubhouse. They told him that with two outs, Cardinal George Watkins had belted a two-strike homer to tie the score and that Frisch had slugged the next pitch onto the roof of the right-field pavilion to win the game 2–1. Grimes had won. Grimes called the victory the most satisfactory of the season, even if he hadn't seen it.

Red Smith, then a reporter in St. Louis, called Frisch's homer "the longest homer in history" because Frisch bragged about it all the way to Boston that night on the train.

Frisch had a lot to brag about in 1931. The Cardinals were overpowering. They won 101 games, losing only 53, and finished 13 games ahead of the second-place Giants. Frankie batted .311, drove in 82 runs and led the league in stolen bases. Then the Cardinals beat the Philadelphia Athletics in the World Series. When the votes were counted for the first Most Valuable Player award, Frankie Frisch was the winner.

In the middle of the 1933 season, he was appointed

player–manager of the Cardinals. His new position, as manager of the "Gas House Gang," was to open a new and fascinating period in Frisch's career. The Cardinals were in the process of acquiring some of baseball's most famous characters. But these men were also fine ballplayers.

The Gas House Gang was scrappy on the field and in the clubhouse. It was rumored that outfielder Ducky Medwick would fight anyone any time and any place. Pitcher Dizzy Dean and outfielder Pepper Martin, two of the club's biggest stars, often wrestled on the cement floor of the clubhouse just for fun. One day when the temperature reached 100 degrees in St. Louis, Dean and Martin wrapped themselves in blankets and set a fire on the dugout floor. They also had ambitions to be racing drivers, hoping to drive in the Indianapolis 500. But they settled for cruising around the streets of St. Louis.

The Gas House Gang was very musical. On overnight train rides they would serenade other passengers with a strange collection of guitars, fiddles and washboards. Or they would arrange a concert in a hotel lobby if the idea suddenly occurred to them.

Frisch's Cardinals were also playful. Martin once threw a box of sneeze powder into a hotel air-conditioning unit. Shortstop Leo Durocher once organized the Gang into a construction crew. They barged into

Frisch scores again for the Cardinals.

The great Cardinal infield: third baseman Pepper Martin, second baseman Frisch, first baseman Jim Collins and shortstop Rogers Hornsby. Hornsby was one of the game's most consistent hitters.

a convention at a hotel, carrying ladders, paint buckets and tools, scattering the convention delegates in all directions.

Frisch led the Cardinals to a pennant in 1934, then

to a hard-fought victory over Detroit in the World Series. In that Series angry Detroit fans showered left fielder Medwick with ripe fruit and harder objects, forcing him to leave the game.

Frisch played until 1937, when his tired legs finally gave out. During his nineteen years as a player, he batted .316 and helped win eight pennants. He managed no more pennant winners after 1934. In 1938 the Cardinals let him go. He later managed at Pittsburgh and Chicago and was a baseball broadcaster in Boston and New York. Frisch also became one of baseball's most famous after-dinner speakers.

"Everybody says I only won the award once," Frankie Frisch recalled recently. "Well, they're right. But they didn't start that award until 1931. If they'd started it earlier, I could have won it two or three times."

Then he added, "If you don't think a player gets a heartfelt kick out of winning the award, you don't know ballplayers."

4
JOE DIMAGGIO

Most Valuable Player, American League,
1939, 1941, 1947

People often talk about a "Yankee type" as if
all the great New York Yankee players looked and
acted the same. The Yankees are always impres-
sive of course, in their pin-striped uniforms, but
no true Yankee fan would claim that Mickey Mantle
with his muscular build, crippling injuries and sulking disposition, really resembles Babe Ruth, with
his slender legs, big belly and noisy disposition.
Yankee stars have come in all different shapes, sizes
and personalities—from Ruth to Mantle.

There was one Yankee, however, who certainly fitted the Yankee image—if there is such a thing. He was tall and graceful, powerful and quiet. And he awed people just by trotting out to his position in center field. His name was Joseph Paul DiMaggio. DiMaggio was nicknamed "The Yankee Clipper," after the proud and graceful sailing ships of the 1800s. Cruising in center field or swinging his bat at home plate, DiMaggio always seemed to resemble the stately ships.

The Yankee Clipper grew up near the port where the real clipper ships once sailed, in the North Beach section of San Francisco. His family owned a fishing boat and all nine children worked on the boat. But Joe's stomach did not take to the high seas, so he had more time for baseball than his brothers.

Baseball had always been a family interest. Before Joe had finished high school, his older brother Vince was the star of the San Francisco Seals in the Pacific Coast League. Occasionally Joe was allowed to work out with the Seals before their games, and before long he had replaced his brother as the star of the team.

In June, 1934, Joe starred in a double-header at Seal Stadium. Too tired to walk home, he took a cab. While riding, he twisted his leg underneath him. When he got home, he paid the driver and stepped out on his left foot. The foot was asleep and wouldn't support his weight. The nineteen-year-old athlete fell to the street, his knee shooting with pain.

The knee was badly torn, and Joe's value as a ballplayer suddenly decreased. Only the Yankees remained interested. They paid the Seals $25,000 for him and then ordered him to sit out the entire 1935 season to let the knee heal properly.

By 1936 DiMaggio was ready to play again. The Yankees had not won a pennant in three years. But DiMaggio batted .323 as a rookie, took over center field and led the Yankees to the flag. He also helped them win pennants in the next three years. He batted .381 in 1939, and in that same season he won his first Most Valuable Player award. The next year, 1940, was quiet. The Yankees didn't win the pennant and Joe's batting average slipped to .352.

Joe got off to a bad start in 1941. He was hitting only .306 in the middle of May, a good average for most players but below par for Joe. The Yankees were in fourth place. A headline in a New York paper said: "YANK ATTACK WEAKEST IN YEARS."

On May 15 DiMaggio slapped a first-inning single off pitcher Edgar Smith of the White Sox. Nobody paid much attention, since the Yankees were bombed, 13–1. But Joe had started on the longest hitting streak in major league baseball.

On May 24, Joe had hit in nine straight games—

DiMaggio shows the graceful form that earned him the name "The Yankee Clipper." He is shown as a rookie in 1936 and as a veteran in 1949.

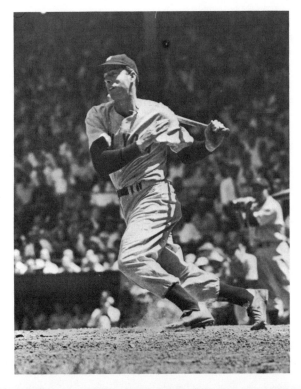

but Yankee opponents still were not concerned. In the game that day against the Red Sox, Joe came up with Yank runners on second and third and the Red Sox ahead by one run. It was a natural situation for an intentional walk but Red Sox manager Joe Cronin told his pitcher to go for the out. DiMaggio singled to win the game. Now he had hit in ten straight games.

Joe had noticed a flaw in his batting stance in late May and corrected it. The hits came easier now. In mid-June he smashed a ground ball that took a bad hop and hit White Sox shortstop Luke Appling on the shoulder. It was only a scratch single but DiMaggio had now hit in twenty-nine straight games —a Yankee record.

Joe's next goal was forty-four straight games, the major league record set by Willie Keeler of the old Baltimore Orioles in 1897. None of his teammates noticed any change in him, though. "To look at Joe," said Yankee pitcher Lefty Gomez, "you'd never think he had any pressure on him. I never saw a guy so calm. *I* wound up with the upset stomachs."

Other teams were trying to stop his streak now. One night he went into the eighth inning without a hit. Manager Luke Sewell of the St. Louis Browns wanted his pitcher, Bob Muncrief, to walk DiMaggio. But Muncrief disobeyed orders and pitched to Di-

Maggio. The Clipper slashed a single. Now he had hit in thirty-six straight games.

"Why didn't you walk him?" Sewell asked Muncrief.

"I wasn't going to walk him," Muncrief said. "That wouldn't have been fair to him or to me. Heck, he's the greatest player I ever saw."

In the thirty-eighth game, DiMaggio was hitless going into the bottom of the eighth inning with the Yankees ahead. He was the fourth man due up in the inning. Fortunately Red Rolfe walked with one out. Then Tommy Henrich sacrificed, to avoid ending the inning with a double play. Joe got his chance, coming up with two out. He doubled to left to keep his streak alive.

In the fortieth game of DiMaggio's hitting streak, the Yankees came up against pitcher Johnny Babich of the Philadelphia Athletics. Babich had beaten the Yankees five times the previous year, helping to ruin their pennant chances. "He was out to stop me," DiMaggio said, "even if it meant walking me every time up."

When Joe came up, Babich threw three straight balls past him. The Yankee bench was furious with Babich. Manager Joe McCarthy signaled DiMaggio to swing on the 3–0 pitch if he liked it. The pitch was high and inside but DiMaggio swung anyway. He hit a line drive that shot right through Babich's legs and out into center field for a double.

"When I got to second base I looked at Babich," DiMaggio said. "He was as white as a ghost."

In Washington the next day, a fan jumped onto the field and stole DiMaggio's lucky bat. With an unfamiliar substitute, Joe hit into three straight outs. Then he remembered that he had loaned another bat just like the lucky one to teammate Tommy Henrich. He reclaimed it and singled to left field in the seventh inning. Now he had a streak of forty-two games.

DiMaggio got his own bat back the next day. The thief had made the mistake of bragging about stealing the bat. Some Yankee fans heard him and reclaimed it for DiMaggio. Joe used the bat to hit in his forty-third and forty-fourth straight games. On July 2 he went after Willie Keeler's major-league record.

The Yanks were playing Boston and the temperature in Yankee Stadium was 95 degrees. DiMaggio had to face a hard-throwing Red Sox rookie named Dick Newsome. He lined out in the first inning. In the third he grounded out. But in the fifth inning, with the count at two balls and one strike, DiMaggio slammed a long fly ball to left field. Everybody in Yankee Stadium watched the ball soar into the left-field stands. It was DiMaggio's eighteenth homer. And he had hit in forty-five straight games. He owned the record now.

On his way to first with a single, Joe increases his 1941 hitting streak to 56 games.

"I'm glad it's over," DiMaggio said. "I don't know how far I can go but I'm not going to worry about it any more. It got to be quite a strain the last ten days."

The strain was over but the streak went on. DiMaggio hit in eleven more games. On July 16 he had three hits against Cleveland in his fifty-sixth game.

The next night on the way to the ball park, a cab driver told DiMaggio, "You know, Joe, I've got the feeling that if you don't get a hit the first time up tonight, it's all over for you."

There were 67,468 fans in Municipal Stadium watching Al Smith pitch to DiMaggio. Third baseman Ken Keltner moved back to the edge of the outfield grass.

"He dared me to bunt on him," DiMaggio said. "I didn't bunt during the entire streak."

With one ball and no strikes DiMaggio smashed the ball toward third. Keltner dove to his right, made a backhand grab of the ball and, from foul territory, threw DiMaggio out at first.

In the fourth inning Smith walked DiMaggio. In the seventh Keltner threw him out again on a hard ground ball. In the eighth Jim Bagby, Jr., was the new pitcher. DiMaggio swung at a 2–1 pitch and hit a sharp grounder to Lou Boudreau at shortstop.

Boudreau made a good catch and flipped to second base to start a double play. "DiMaggio rounded first base, picked up his glove and trotted to center field," wrote Herb Goren in the New York *Sun* the next day. "There was no kicking of dirt, no shaking of the head."

DiMaggio didn't come up again that game and his hitting streak was over at 56 games. Nobody has ever approached that record. During his streak he drove in 55 runs, scored 56 more and made 91 hits including 15 home runs.

The streak did wonders for his batting average. He finished the season with a .357 average and the Yankees won the 1941 pennant and the World Series. DiMaggio was once again named Most Valuable Player.

After the 1942 season he went into the Army. Joe served in the armed forces three years, during which the Yankees won only one pennant. Returning in 1946, he had some trouble adjusting to baseball. He batted only .290 and the Yankees lost another pennant. But in 1947 he snapped back, batting .315 and leading the Yankees to another world championship. For the third time Joe was named Most Valuable Player.

Joe always seemed to be making a comeback from some injury. The year after his third Most Valuable Player award, he suffered a heel injury and needed an operation. He was still hobbling when the 1949 season began. Many people, including DiMaggio,

Despite aches and pains, Joe slams into the catcher in a 1948 game to score another run for the Yanks.

had reason to think that he was nearing the end of his career.

DiMaggio rested in his New York apartment that spring. He didn't go to the ball park because there was nothing he could do there. Every time he took his foot out of bed, the stabbing pain in his heel would start again. "Then one morning I rolled out of bed and started to put on my socks," he recalls. "There was no pain. It was like a miracle."

The Yankees had a pleasant sight that afternoon.

DiMaggio put on a uniform and took batting practice for the first time in three months. But he was careful not to overdo it.

On June 27 DiMaggio finally decided he was ready. The Yankees were playing the Giants for the Mayor's Trophy. It was a good chance to thrill the fans and get a workout at the same time. DiMaggio was supposed to play only a few innings. But he felt so good that he played the whole game.

The next night the Yankees began a three-game series in Boston. DiMaggio decided to play. In the third inning, with Phil Rizzuto on first base, DiMaggio swung at a fastball and the ball disappeared into the center-field stands. The Yankees won, 5–2.

"DiMag was really happy after that game," Yogi Berra recalls. "He wasn't the kind of guy to show it much, but you could tell it meant a lot to him to be playing again and doing something to help the club . . ."

The next day DiMaggio felt well enough to play again. The Yankees were trailing, 7–1, in the fifth inning. Then DiMaggio came up with two men on base. When he slugged a three-run homer over Boston's left-field wall, even the Boston fans cheered. They had always liked DiMaggio and figured it was safe to cheer for him when Boston had a 7–4 lead.

But their good nature didn't last. Gene Woodling

hit a three-run double to tie the score, 7–7, in the seventh inning. Then in the eighth inning DiMaggio batted again. He slugged his second homer of the game and the Yankees went on to win, 9–7.

In the third game the Yankees managed to take a 3-2 lead in the seventh inning. Then DiMaggio came up with two men on. The Clipper had already belted three homers in two days. You couldn't expect much more from a man who had been out of commission for three months. But DiMaggio took his smooth swing at a 3–2 pitch and the ball floated over the left-field wall again. The Yankees won, 6–3.

Back in the clubhouse, DiMaggio was smiling broadly, although he wasn't talking much. He had hit four homers in his first three games. He didn't need to talk. The rest of the Yankees made the noise. They sang a song written a few years earlier: "Joe, Joe, DiMaggio, we want you on our side."

He was quite a man to have on your side. During the Clipper's 13 seasons with the Yankees, they won 10 pennants. Even in his last year, batting only .263 in 72 games, he was the star. But he knew it was time to retire.

"I had a bad year. I guess the reflexes just weren't there," he said. It was a sad day when Joe announced his retirement. People said the Yankees would never be the same.

But even after Joe DiMaggio retired, the Yankees retained his style. They remembered his proud, silent manner and they imitated it. Nobody was more like DiMaggio in that respect than Mickey Mantle, who inherited center field from the Yankee Clipper. Years later, the DiMaggio spirit still made itself felt in the Yankee clubhouse and on the field as the team won pennant after pennant, quietly and gracefully.

5
STAN MUSIAL

Most Valuable Player, National League,
1943, 1946, 1948

Nobody in baseball has anything unkind to say about
Stan Musial. Almost everybody makes an enemy
sooner or later, particularly a man who has murdered
National League pitching for twenty-two years. But
Musial, with his lopsided grin and quick giggle, was
popular with all baseball fans. He was even popular
in Brooklyn.

This may not sound so amazing today. There hasn't
been a team in Brooklyn since 1957, when the Dodgers
moved to Los Angeles. But the old Dodger fans in

50

Brooklyn were the toughest in baseball. Ebbets Field, where the Dodgers played, was small and noises carried. Fans could practically boo a man out of the park if they wanted to. They sometimes carried over-ripe fruit to throw at Dodger opponents. Their targets were close and their aim was good.

Stan Musial, a St. Louis Cardinal, should have been the ideal target for the treatment. He was rough enough on the Dodgers in St. Louis, but in Ebbets Field he was brutal. In 1948 he batted .545 against the Dodgers. Even his outs were line drives.

The Cardinals came to Ebbets Field that summer for a two-game series. In the first game Musial hit a triple, a double and three singles and walked once. In the second game he hit a homer, two doubles and a single.

For any other visiting player this would have been a dangerous performance. But Musial seemed so friendly as he trotted around the bases that even Dodger fans couldn't hate him. When the Cardinals played in Brooklyn the next time, Dodger fans just groaned. "Stan the Man" was back in town.

Soon Brooklyn rooters settled on a wonderful plan. The Dodgers should buy Musial from the Cardinals. It was a magnificent idea. But, unsurprisingly, Musial was never for sale. Stan was special in St. Louis, too. His name was almost as famous as the name of the team and every fan in St. Louis knew the story of how he had almost given up baseball in 1940.

Musial had been a pitcher in the minor leagues. Then he injured his shoulder and couldn't throw his sizzling fastball any more. He decided to quit baseball. But his manager, Dickie Kerr, a former major league pitcher recognized a potential major leaguer when he saw one. "You can't quit, Stan," Kerr said. "You have the makings of a great hitter. Give yourself time."

Musial finally listened to Kerr and stayed in baseball. Concentrating on hitting and playing the outfield, he became the star of three minor leagues in two years. The Cardinals called him up for the last two weeks of the 1941 season.

People were not impressed with Musial when he reported to the Cardinals. They made fun of his odd batting stance. He twisted his body like a corkscrew, so that his right ear, right shoulder and right hip were facing the pitcher. It was described as a "peeking-around-the-corner" style. No one understood how he could even swing the bat.

Musial's first major league game was against the Boston Braves. A crafty veteran named Jim Tobin was pitching. He threw Musial a knuckleball and Musial popped to third base. The next time, Tobin tried another knuckler and Musial slashed a double

Stan Musial scores again against the helpless Dodgers. Dodger catcher Roy Campanella waits for the throw.

to right field. He was on his way.

"Throw him the snake," shouted the Boston manager, Casey Stengel, who later managed the Yankees and Mets. Tobin threw a few "snakes," baseball's term for a curveball. But Musial uncoiled himself from his strange stance and straightened them out. Soon even Stengel was convinced.

"They've got another one," Stengel muttered.

Stengel, trying to manage a poor team like the Braves, didn't think it fair that the Cardinals should get all the good players. The Cardinals already had a whole team of stars. But the best of them all was the one-time minor league pitcher, Stan Musial.

Musial hit .426 in the last two weeks of 1941, too late to help the Cardinals, who finished behind the Dodgers. But the Cardinals won the pennant the next three years in a row. In 1942 Musial batted .315. The other players in the league had to admit that his corkscrew batting stance worked. But they soon learned that they could tease him about it.

"Why don't you take lessons from the batting coach?" his teammates would shout when he took batting practice.

"Do you think it would help?" Musial would answer with a big grin.

"You're never going to make it," an opponent would shout.

Stan demonstrates his "corkscrew" stance—knees together, bat held far in back of him, "peeking" over his shoulder at the pitcher.

"I'd better find another line of work," Musial would say. Then he would break into his familiar giggle.

Musial always seemed to be laughing—often at himself. He was not the kind of ballplayer to make stirring speeches in the clubhouse. He sat with rookies in the back of the bus and took batting practice when his turn came. He was always just one of the team. Only his batting average was different.

In 1943 Musial batted .357 and was named the Most Valuable Player in the league. Neither the batting average nor the award made any difference in his personality.

"Stan never changed," said Butch Yatkeman, the long-time clubhouse man. "There was no difference between Musial the rookie and Musial the star. In all my years with the club I never heard him ask for a favor—and never heard him turn one down."

Musial was embarrassed by attention. When fans sent him gifts, he had the clubhouse man pass them out to the rookies. When reporters praised his hitting, he praised his teammates.

"Musial is the greatest player of our time," said Eddie Stanky, who managed the Cardinals from 1952 to 1955. "He used to make it easy for me by always being on time, not taking extra swings in batting practice, not flying ahead of the club. In other words he never sought the extra privileges often demanded by top stars to the detriment of team morale."

After winning the pennant in each of Musial's first three seasons, the Cardinals lost it in 1945. Musial was in the Navy that year. He came back in 1946 to bat .365 and the Cardinals won the pennant and the World Series. He was named Most Valuable Player again.

In 1947 Musial suffered from appendicitis all season and required constant medication until doctors could operate in October. The Cardinals fell to second place and Stan batted a weak .312.

The Man recovered again in 1948. He had his greatest season and the Cardinals needed every base hit of it. Their pitching suddenly folded and Musial had to carry them with his bat. He did the best he could. He was hitting about .370 as the season entered September. But the Braves stayed ahead of St. Louis in a tight pennant race.

The Cardinals went on an eastern road trip that was expected to decide the pennant. The first stop was Brooklyn. In the first game Musial took a vicious spill while chasing a fly ball and wrenched his arm. Although he was in pain, he continued to play.

In the bottom of the ninth inning, with the score tied, the Dodgers got a runner to second base with one out. The dangerous Pistol Pete Reiser was up. Before Reiser could bat, however, Musial came trotting in from the outfield to talk to manager Eddie Dyer.

"I know I'm up first in the tenth," Musial said, "but if Reiser hits a ground ball out there, I don't think I can make the throw to the plate with my arm the way it is. Better take me out."

Dyer knew that Musial wanted to bat in the tenth. But he also knew there wouldn't be any tenth inning if they didn't get the Dodgers out now. So he sent a replacement to the outfield. Reiser slapped a single and the run scored anyway. But Dyer and others were impressed with Musial's thoughtfulness.

The next stop on the road trip was Boston. In the first game Musial was hit on the wrist with a pitch. Now he had two injuries. He looked bad at bat in the first game.

"I don't think I'll do much out there today," Musial told a friend before the second game. "My arm and wrist feel bad. Even taping them doesn't seem to help."

On his first trip to the plate Musial held the bat loosely and slapped a single to right field. He held the bat a little tighter the next time up and whacked a double to deep center. The third time up he swung hard and hit a homer. By his fourth time at bat, however, the wrist was beginning to ache. But he poked a single anyway.

By now Musial was in real pain. But the Cardinals still needed him in the game. The fifth time up he could only slap at the ball. He slapped a ground single between second and third base for his fifth hit. Despite two painful injuries, he had tied a major league record by making five hits in a game for the fourth time that season.

"He's spoiled me," said Bob Bauman, the team's trainer. "I expect everybody to be like him but nobody can. He never complained. He had the greatest tolerance of pain of any man I ever knew. He played at times when lesser men would have folded."

The Cardinals lost the 1948 pennant to the Braves. But Musial batted .376 with 131 runs batted in and 39 homers. He led the league in batting average, runs scored, hits, doubles, triples and runs batted in. He was second in home runs. His clutch performances were too good to be ignored. For the third time in his career, Musial was voted Most Valuable Player.

The record books say that 1948 was Musial's finest season. He played for fifteen more years, however, and some people think that the 1963 season was just as great. By that time Musial was 42 years old. He announced in August that he would retire after the season. Every city announced a special going-away party for him in his last trip around the league.

But this was no time for sentiment. Late in the season, the Cardinals suddenly got hot and won 19 of 20 games, catching up with the league-leading Los Angeles Dodgers. One of the best hitters during

Stan accepts the congratulations of MVP Ken Boyer after hitting his third homer in one game in 1962.

the Cardinal streak was the 42-year-old Stan the Man.

"He astounded me during the last thirty days of the season," said manager Johnny Keane. "The way he responded despite aches and pains and obvious weariness. . . . During our surge he kept getting key hits that either tied the score or put us ahead. Every day I'd say to myself, 'He can't do it again, but he did—through some superhuman effort. I wanted to rest him but I didn't dare because I knew if I did, I'd be hurting the team."

In September the Dodgers came to Busch Stadium in St. Louis for a three-game series. The Cardinals were only one game behind; first place was riding on every game. This made the pressure intense as 32,442 fans packed the old ball park. In the first game, the Dodgers scored a run in the sixth inning. Then in the bottom of the seventh, the 42-year-old Musial hit a home run over the right-field pavilion. The score was tied at 1–1.

The Cards lost the game, 3–1, in the ninth inning and they lost the next two games, too. But Musial had done his share. In the three games he had four hits in ten times at bat—not bad for somebody about to become a grandfather.

During the last two weeks Musial waved good-bye to all his fans. In the last game of his career, in front of tearful St. Louis fans, Musial made two hits, just as he had done in his first game, 3,026 games earlier.

"No improvement," wrote one reporter. It was hard to imagine Stan being better than he was—as a hitter or as a man.

6
LOU BOUDREAU

Most Valuable Player, American League, 1948

Lou Boudreau was home in Illinois in 1941 when he heard that the Cleveland Indians were seeking a new manager. This was important news to the dark-eyed, dark-haired Boudreau, for he was the star 24-year-old shortstop of the Indians.

Boudreau knew the Indians needed a good manager. He had seen them falter in 1940 and 1941 because they weren't getting along with the ones they had. In 1940 the older players had revolted against Oscar Vitt, who continually picked on them.

The Indians finished second and Vitt was fired after the season.

In 1941 the Indian manager was an older man named Roger Peckinpaugh. He was so mild and the players were so content that they loafed all the way to fourth place. So after the 1941 season Peckinpaugh was moved to an office job and the club owner, Alva Bradley, was looking for a new manager.

Boudreau had always been a leader. During the off-season he had been helping coach the basketball team at the University of Illinois. A few years earlier he had been the star play-maker there. He had been elected team captain as a junior and had won All-America honors as a senior. When he was only thirteen years old, he had helped coach a grammar school team. In high school he sparked Harvey High into the Illinois state championship. And in two years with Cleveland he had taken command of the Indians' infield.

Boudreau had always felt he could handle men. And the more he thought about the need for a new Indian manager, the more he said: "Why not me?" He picked up the phone and called Alva Bradley. "I'd like to come to Cleveland and talk to you about the manager's job," he said. "I think I can handle it."

Bradley was too amazed to argue and he even agreed to consider Boudreau. As soon as he had

A good hitter and a great shortstop, Boudreau risked losing his playing talent by trying to manage at the same time.

hung up the phone, however, he thought of several good reasons why Boudreau should not be manager. First, Lou was too young. Had anyone ever heard of a 24-year-old manager in the major leagues? Second, Lou had no experience managing professional players. Third, his playing would suffer. Lou was the best shortstop in the league and he could scarcely be expected to stay in top form and manage at the same time. Bradley assumed that everyone else would think the idea was ridiculous, too.

The next day Bradley played golf with 83-year-old George Martin, a member of the team's board of directors. As they trudged down the fairway, Bradley casually mentioned that young Lou Boudreau had volunteered to manage the team. Bradley expected the older man to laugh at the idea. But Martin didn't.

"He's practically been the manager all along," Martin said. "Besides, he has been the captain or leader of every team he played on. Alva, the boy's a natural."

Bradley tried to protest. "Boudreau is the greatest shortstop in the world," Bradley said. "I'm not going to ruin his career by burdening him with the problem of managing. I think he's too young."

Martin was 83 years old, so to him everybody was young. Besides, Martin argued, Boudreau was extremely popular in Cleveland. His exciting play at shortstop had been one of the few bright spots in the 1940 and 1941 seasons. Martin, in fact, was one of Boudreau's greatest fans.

Bradley knew when he was beaten. "All right,"

he muttered, his enthusiasm for the golf game finished. "We'll hire Boudreau—if we can hire some older coaches to protect him." They rushed back to the Indian office and placed a call to Boudreau at the University.

Boudreau was running up and down the basketball court with a whistle in his mouth when he was told that there was a long- distance call for him. It was Alva Bradley. "Get down here on the first possible train," Bradley said.

The next night Boudreau was introduced as the new Indian manager—the youngest manager in the history of the major leagues. Reporters wasted no time giving him a nickname—"The Boy Wonder." But many of them disagreed with the choice. "Oh, great," a Cleveland reporter wrote. "They get a Baby Snooks for a manager and ruin the best shortstop in baseball."

The entire baseball world was watching Boudreau during spring training of 1942. He was trying to instill "college spirit" into his players. Boudreau reminded them that they were representing a city and a team. They should be gentlemen at all times. But many observers doubted that the 24-year-old manager could handle the club.

When spring training ended, the Indians headed north, playing a series of exhibition games on their

Twenty-four-year-old Boudreau consults with his team before the opening game of the 1942 season.

way back to Cleveland. One day as the train clacked its way through the South, the players were eating dinner in the dining car. Boudreau was sitting with his coaches.

Suddenly some horseplay started when one player threw a hard roll at another. The second man dumped a glass of water on the first man's head. They began elbowing each other and the other players laughed. Everybody had one eye on Boudreau, to see how he would handle the situation. If he couldn't stop the horseplay, it would be the signal for a hundred other such incidents to erupt. Most of the men were older than he, so Lou would have to show that he was the boss.

Boudreau didn't even stand up. "All right," he barked. "That's enough. Now sit down, both of you, before I have to pass out some fines." The two players sat down and stopped shoving. It was clear to everyone that the Boy Wonder meant business.

But as the season began Boudreau was still on trial. He had picked the worst possible time to become manager. World War II had begun during the winter and most of the able-bodied men had joined the armed forces. Cleveland's Bobby Feller, the best pitcher of the era, had gone into the Navy. The only Indian star left was Boudreau. He was not called up because of arthritic ankles, weakened by years of pounding on the basketball courts.

Boudreau was one of baseball's biggest stars during the war. He did much to maintain interest in the sport while far more serious matters were happening overseas. But during the war years the Indians finished in fourth, third and fifth (twice) place. Boudreau had still not proved himself as a top-rate manager.

The war ended late in 1945 and the players started to trickle back. One man who returned was Bill Veeck, a baseball executive who was looking for a team to buy and operate. Veeck had been painfully injured during the war—most of one leg would eventually have to be amputated. But he limped into Cleveland in 1946 and bought the Indians from Alva Bradley.

It was an exciting time for the city. Veeck was a showman who believed in giving the fans a good time. He would give away live chickens or fresh orchids as door prizes, set off fireworks, and present music or clowns between innings. He was determined to keep the fans happy and to keep them coming back to the park. But he wanted the best team in baseball, too.

Veeck was also a direct person. He called Boudreau into his office and told him: "You probably want to know exactly where you stand, Lou. Well, we're going to be very frank with you. We know all about your ball playing. You're the best, and that's putting it mildly. But we have some doubts about your managing ability."

Although Veeck said nothing about changing managers immediately, it was clear that Lou was on trial. He knew that if he didn't produce a winner or at least a near-winner soon, he might be looking for another job.

Boudreau's contribution in 1946 was the Boudreau Shift. Boston Red Sox slugger Ted Williams nearly always pulled the ball to right field. Boudreau, tired of being beaten by the Boston star, shifted all his fielders toward the right side of the field. The first baseman moved over near the first baseline, and the second baseman played halfway between first and second. The shortstop played near second base, and the third baseman played between second and third. The outfield was shifted the same way. This plan gave Williams a chance to hit consistently through the unguarded left side of the field. But he believed he could help his team more by staying with his natural swing. Since Williams continued to hit into the Boudreau Shift, the maneuver remained so effective that other teams adopted it. Veeck was impressed with Boudreau's idea.

When Boudreau was omitted from the All-Star

team in July, Veeck's temper flared. He staged a
"night" for Boudreau and called it "A Night for the
Greatest Shortstop Ever Left off the All-Star Team."
Although the situation between Veeck and Boudreau
remained friendly in 1946 and 1947, the Indians
finished in sixth and in fourth place. Veeck became
serious about appointing a new manager. He began
negotiations to trade Boudreau to the St. Louis
Browns for Vern Stephens, a slugging shortstop. He
felt that with Stephens he would have almost as
good a shortstop and would be able to find a better
manager.

But Veeck had never been able to keep a secret
and soon word of the trade leaked out to the Cleveland papers. They ran big headlines: "VEECK TO
TRADE BOUDREAU!" and the next day Veeck
was deluged by calls and telegrams. "Don't come
back if you fire Boudreau," one wire read.

Veeck had to reconsider. IIe discovered that he
was only the second most popular sports figure in
Cleveland. Boudreau was first. So Veeck rehired
Boudreau for another year. When the 1948 season
began, Boudreau and Veeck were barely on speak-
ing terms. Boudreau knew that, despite his popularity in Cleveland, he had only one more season
to prove himself.

It was a good year for the Indians. In fact for

many players it was the best year of their careers. But the star of the team was its 31-year-old shortstop and manager, Lou Boudreau.

By August the American League pennant race was extremely close. The Indians led, but the Yankees, the Athletics and the Red Sox still had a chance to snare the flag. Then Gil Coan of Washington slid hard into Boudreau at second base and injured him. Boudreau missed a few games and didn't think he could play in an important twinight double-header against the Yankees.

There were 73,484 fans in Municipal Stadium that night, but Boudreau was on the bench nursing his injuries. The Yankees had a 6–1 lead in the seventh inning and things looked bad for the Indians. But the Cleveland team scored three times in the last of the seventh and loaded the bases. Thurman Tucker was due to bat, but the fans in the huge stadium were not roaring for him. They screamed and pointed to the dugout, where Boudreau was fumbling for the right bat.

Taped from shoulder to foot ("like a mummy," wrote one sports writer), Boudreau limped to home plate. His right thumb was so tender that he could not hold it against the bat. His legs were so sore that he could not dig in with his spikes.

The fans roared as Boudreau waved the bat and

the pitcher wound up. Boudreau swung—and smashed a line-drive single to center. Two runs scored and the game was tied. Eddie Robinson hit a homer in the eighth inning to win the game for Cleveland. The Indians also won the second game.

The Boy Wonder was getting old. He didn't recover from injuries as quickly as he had in previous seasons. But he struggled back into the line-up as the last furious days of the pennant race approached. The Indians were behind, then ahead. They lost on the last day of the season to finish in a tie with Boston. This set up the first play-off game in the history of the American League.

The Indians had run out of pitchers. "We're all in this together," Boudreau said. "It's your money as well as mine. If you have any ideas of your own, speak up."

"We've gone along all season with you, Lou," said the second baseman, Joe Gordon. "That's been good enough for me. I think we'd be crazy not to go along with you for this big one." Boudreau looked around and saw twenty-five players nodding. They had faith in their manager.

Boudreau started Gene Bearden in the big game, and he made sure his pitcher had the proper support. Lou hit a home run in the first inning and the Indians led, 1–0. He singled in the fourth and Ken

Even Indian owner Bill Veeck (circled) applauds when Boudreau comes back to the dugout after his second home run of the play-off game.

Keltner hit a three-run homer. The Indians led, 4–1. Boudreau hit another homer in the fifth, and in the ninth inning he singled to set up the final run. Lou had four hits in the biggest game of the season to help Gene Bearden beat the Red Sox, 8–3.

The Boy Wonder was a pennant-winning manager now. He was also a .355 hitter. He led the Indians into the World Series and Cleveland beat the Braves in six games. On the train going back to Cleveland after the last series game, the Indian players toasted Lou Boudreau who, as a fielder, a hitter and a manager, had led them to a world championship. They cheered all the way back to Cleveland.

Later that fall Boudreau was given a new contract by Veeck. "Lou was determined to prove I was a jerk," Veeck said. "I was. He did. So he won the championship and he gets a new contract."

And in November Boudreau was voted the Most Valuable Player in the American League. He received 22 out of 24 first-place votes. Only two die-hard New York reporters held out for Joe DiMaggio.

It was a great year for Boudreau. But his success didn't last. The Indians slipped out of first place in 1949, and Veeck sold the team in 1950. Boudreau lasted one more year under the new owners. His playing suffered as he grew older and his managing didn't seem quite so adept. He retired as a player and moved on to manage the Red Sox, the Cubs and the Kansas City Athletics. But he never won another pennant.

In 1960 Boudreau left the playing field to become a broadcaster for the Chicago Cubs. Now he wears business suits and sits in the announcing booth. But to a whole generation of fans he is still the 24-year-old shortstop who called up Alva Bradley and said, "Why not me?"

7

TED WILLIAMS

Most Valuable Player, American League, 1946, 1949

The Boston Red Sox outfielders laughed when Ted Williams was sent to the minor leagues in the spring of 1938. They had heard how good he was and were glad to see him fail in his first tryout with the team.

"So long, busher," they jeered. They were sure they would never again see the nineteen-year-old from San Diego, California.

"I'll be back," Williams assured them. "And someday I'll be making more money than all three of you." He roared back in the spring of 1939 and he still thought he was the greatest. This time he made the team. In his first trip to the plate in the major leagues, he watched Red Ruffing of the Yankees strike him out on a change-up pitch. Ruffing was one of the top pitchers in the league.

"If he throws me that again, I'll knock it out of the park," Williams vowed. Ruffing immediately threw it again. Williams didn't knock it out of the park—but he slashed a double into the right-field corner.

Ted Williams stood out, right from the start. He was bigger than most players, at a height of six-foot-four and a weight of 225 pounds. He was dark and handsome, in a rough, manly way. Usually he was happy, and the other players could hear his laughter across a ball field. When he was mad, though, his rough words boomed through the club-house.

"All I want out of life," he once said, "is to be able to walk down the street and have people point at me and say, 'There goes the greatest hitter who ever lived.'" By his third season, 1941, people were suggested that Theodore Samuel Williams might be as good as he said.

Williams went into the last day of the 1941 season with exactly a .400 average. It was an amazing average for any hitter, and it was almost incredible for a player in his third major league season. If he took the day off, Williams would have his .400 for all time. If he played, he took the chance of losing it. The Red Sox' last double-header against Philadelphia was unimportant. The Yankees had already wrapped up another pennant and neither Boston nor Philadelphia was in contention.

Manager Joe Cronin wanted to see Williams keep his .400 average. Before the game he edged over to the locker where Williams was putting on his uniform. "Do you want to sit it out?" he said.

"Heck, no," Williams replied. "If I'm going to be a champion, I'm going to act like one."

Williams continued to dress. He knew the fans were streaming into the ball park to witness his struggle for .400. If he chose to sit in the dugout all day, he knew the fans would accuse him of having no courage. More important, Williams knew he would accuse himself of having no courage. So he picked up a few bats and began his long-legged stride out to the field.

The fans roared when Williams stepped into the batter's box in the first inning. He planted his feet exactly 24 inches apart and took a few menacing left-handed practice swings. Then he heard the voice of the Philadelphia catcher, Frankie Hayes.

Williams swings in practice during the 1941 season. His .406 batting average that season has not been equaled since.

"I wish you all the luck in the world, Ted," Hayes said. "But Mr. Mack told us he'd run us out of baseball if we let up on you. You're going to have to earn it."

Williams nodded. He knew that the Philadelphia manager, frail old Connie Mack, sitting in street clothes in the Athletic's dugout, would make things as tough as possible. Williams proceeded to lash a single to right field. His next time up he hit a home run. Then he hit two singles.

In the second game he whacked two more hits. Although he had Cronin's permission to quit at any time, he played both games and batted .750 for the day against the best pitchers Mr. Mack could find. The season was over and Ted Williams had made himself a .406 hitter. No major leaguer—not even Joe DiMaggio or Stan Musial—has ever hit .400 for a full season since 1941. Some baseball experts think nobody will ever do it again.

Williams' average fell all the way to .356 in 1942. Then he enlisted in the Marines to participate in World War II. He served as a flight instructor for the next three years. Williams was discharged from the Marines before the 1946 season and continued where he had left off four years earlier. He batted .342 and led the Red Sox to their first pennant in twenty-eight years.

Williams was so good in 1946 that other managers tried extra hard to stop him. Lou Boudreau, the player-manager of Cleveland, even invented the "Boudreau Shift" between games of a double-header in 1946 in an attempt to stop Williams. Ted had hit three homers in the first game and Boston had won, 11–0.

This shift put extra fielders where Williams normally pulled the ball. But it left a huge gap in left field. Boudreau was daring Williams to slap the ball to left field. If he did, he would be able to hit singles and doubles, but would be robbed of his power. Williams was stubborn, however. He felt that he was most valuable when he took his natural swing at the ball. So he refused to change his style because of the shift and continued to pull the ball into right field. This cost him countless hits but nobody could stop Williams for long. He still compiled one of the highest batting averages in baseball history.

Williams was the star of the 1946 All-Star Game. He had four hits in four times at bat. The last time up, he faced Rip Sewell of Pittsburgh, who threw an "eephus pitch," a lob pitch that arched 25 feet into the air and came almost straight down into the strike zone. It was very hard to hit. Williams wound up and waited for the dead ball to float down. When it arrived, he slugged a 400-foot homer. He always remembered that hit as one of his favorites.

The Red Sox had jumped into first place early in the 1946 season and stayed there all the way. They clinched the pennant in mid-September. In the deciding game, Williams hit an inside-the- park homer in the first inning, for the Red Sox' only run. Tex Hughson pitched a 1–0 shutout.

Williams hurt his elbow in the last week of the season. Bothered by the sore elbow during the Series, Williams refused to swing for left field against the Cardinals' Boudreau Shift and hit only five singles in 25 times at bat, a .200 average. He drove in only one run and the Red Sox lost the Series to the Cardinals in seven games.

But Williams had batted the Red Sox to the pennant, and the baseball writers voted Williams the American League's Most Valuable Player for 1946.

He came close to winning the award again in 1947. He won the Triple Crown, leading the league in batting average, home runs and runs batted in. But Joe DiMaggio led the Yankees to another pennant and was voted Most Valuable Player.

In 1948 Williams batted .369. The Red Sox wound up tied with Cleveland for first place. In the first play-off game in American League history, the Indians beat the Red Sox, 8–3, to win the pennant and Williams had just one hit. The Indians' Lou Boudreau had four hits and was voted Most Valuable Player.

In 1949 Williams batted .343 and sparked a late-season drive with some fantastic clutch hitting. The Red Sox won nine straight games in September, including three from the Yankees. Williams beat Hal Newhouser of Detroit, 1–0, with a homer, beat Steve Gromek of Cleveland with a homer, beat Ed Lopat of the Yankees with a homer, and beat Allie Reynolds of the Yankees with a homer. These were four of the league's best pitchers.

The Red Sox led the Yankees by one game with only two games remaining. They met in Yankee Stadium on the last Saturday and Sunday of the season. If the Boston team won either game, they had the pennant. But the Yankees won on Saturday, 5–4. And on Sunday the Yankees' Jerry Coleman chopped a three-run double, giving the Yankees the game, 5–3, and the pennant. Williams didn't have a hit in either game.

Williams was not very valuable to the Red Sox in the last two games. Just one hit in either game would probably have won the pennant. He had led the Red Sox to within one game of the pennant, however, so he was voted Most Valuable Player again in 1949.

Some fans and writers criticized the choice this time. They said that Williams was a great hitter only in unimportant games and didn't care if the Red Sox lost, as long as he made his two hits. The critics said he loafed in the field and on the base paths.

Somebody noted that Williams had batted only .205 in the ten biggest games of his career: the seven World Series games in 1946, the play-off in 1948 and the last two games of 1949. One year, when Williams was hurt, the Red Sox actually played better ball without him than they played with him. That was strange, considering that Williams was a player with a .344 lifetime average, the fourth best since 1900.

Williams brought much of the criticism upon himself. He scolded the fans when they booed him. Several times he made abusive gestures to spectators in Fenway Park. He avoided public appearances and refused to wear a tie. He never tipped his cap when he hit a home run.

"I made up my mind in 1940 never to tip my cap to the fans," he said. "I'll never forget that game. I struck out and followed with an error in the field. Then I really heard it. When I came into the dugout, I swore I'd never tip my cap again, no matter how much I was cheered."

Williams argued with sports writers and may have cost himself votes when they elected the Most Valuable Player. But despite this he received the award twice. If he hadn't made enemies among the writers, Williams might have been elected five times—more than any other player in history. He lost by only a few votes in 1941, 1947 and 1957. But few could deny that he was a great hitter and that he helped the Red Sox despite his feuds with fans and writers.

In 1966, the baseball writers gave Williams another vote of approval. In the first election in which he was eligible, Williams was chosen by an overwhelming majority of the writers for membership in the Baseball Hall of Fame in Cooperstown, New York. Despite his sometimes abrasive temperament, it was clear that he belonged with the greatest of baseball's heroes.

There was another side to Williams, too. He was popular with the fans in Boston. They cheered him and shuddered to think how dull the Red Sox would have been without him. The Red Sox won only one pennant in seventeen years with Williams playing. But at least they were close most of the time. Without Williams they might have finished in the second division.

Williams was also popular with many of his teammates. He would often give batting tips to those who asked for help. A visitor to the Boston clubhouse once said, "I just saw Williams talking to three rookies about hitting. It was like their first day in school."

Birdie Tebbetts, a teammate of Williams at one time and later an opposing manager, called him "the best player I have ever seen . . . an outstanding team

player . . . a great man at the plate in the clutch . . .
not demanding on his teammates . . . highly popular
. . . the best left fielder in the game."

The Boston clubhouse boy will never forget Williams after the 1946 World Series. Williams signed
over his entire World Series check to the boy. The
check was for $2,077.06—the largest single tip in the
history of baseball.

And Williams was generous with his time and
money outside of baseball. There is a charity in
Boston called the Jimmy Fund, which pays for
research into children's diseases and has saved the
lives of many children. Williams was the strongest
supporter the Jimmy Fund ever had. He visited
hospitals regularly, signed hundreds of autographs
for the children, badgered people into contributing
money and gave money himself. But he insisted upon
privacy.

"I've seen Ted with our children," said Dr. Sidney
Farber of the Jimmy Fund. "He comes in quietly to
visit. He comes without publicity. . . . When you put
together all the things that Ted has done, quietly and
earnestly, for other people, it's then that you find a
wonderful human being who has done much good."

Ted also attended Little League World Series for
years at Williamsport. He refused to attend dinners,
to speak or to go to the adult functions and picnics.

After returning from Korea, Williams spent some of his best years with the Red Sox.

But he always made it a point to have dinner with the kids in their mess hall. He talked to them, answered their questions and always brought gifts.

In 1951, Williams' career was interrupted again when he was called to serve in the Korean war. He returned near the end of the 1953 season. He returned to spend some of his happiest years in Boston. He was 35 years old, the Red Sox were not even a first-division club by then and Williams wasn't expected to perform miracles. He lasted seven more years, thrilling Red Sox fans with his hitting. In 1957, when he was thirty-nine years old, Williams led the league with a .388 average.

By this time he was the highest-paid player in baseball. His salary was $125,000 a year—a tribute to his great skill and his popularity with his supporters, who often drove hundreds of miles to see him play. He had kept his word to the three players who had laughed at him in 1938.

But all good things have to come to an end. Williams announced in 1960, at the age of forty-two, that he would retire after the season to spend more time fishing, his favorite pastime.

The weather was damp and chilly on September 28, 1960, but 10,454 fans came to Fenway Park anyway. They were there to watch Ted Williams' last home game and they were rooting for one last homer.

It didn't look as if he would make it. Baltimore's Steve Barber walked him on four pitches in the first inning. Williams flied out in the third. In the fifth inning he backed the right fielder up against the 380-foot sign for a long, long out. Then it was the eighth inning—time for Williams' last swing in Boston.

The new Baltimore pitcher was Jack Fisher, a burly young right-hander. Fisher threw one ball. Williams swung viciously and the crowd groaned as he missed. He didn't miss on the next swing. Everybody knew right away—this was home run number 521, a long fly ball over the centerfield fence. Only Jimmy Foxx with 534 and Babe Ruth with 714 had ever hit more.

Williams circled the bases as he always had before: head down as if he were anxious to get back to the dugout. He didn't tip his hat to the crowd. Although they cheered for minutes after he disappeared into the dugout, he would not appear again to acknowledge the ovation. Even the umpires urged him to return, but he refused.

At the beginning of the ninth inning, Williams went out to left field and the cheering started again. Then he was replaced and he jogged off the field for the last time, still refusing to acknowledge the thousands of his fans. Writer John Updike said of this last appearance, "It was nice and we were grateful, but it left a funny taste."

Head down, Williams comes into home for the last time. He has just hit his 521st home run.

It was all Ted Williams could do. He could hit home runs and be a great hitter. He could be a hero to crippled children or a teacher to rookies in privacy. But he could not tip his cap for the fans and he could not lead his team to a dozen pennants. Although most people agreed that he was great, he was somehow great and disappointing, at the same time.

8
JIM KONSTANTY

Most Valuable Player, National League, 1950

When Jim Konstanty was 31 years old, he heard that
the Philadelphia Phillies were interested in him. He
laughed out loud. "Who would want me, at my age?"
he asked.

When Jim heard about Philadelphia's interest, he
was pitching for Toronto in the International League.
He had pitched for Cincinnati and Boston during
World War II. But when the younger men came back
from the Army, Konstanty had been sent back to the
minor leagues. Now it was 1948.

92

Although he was a big man, at a height of six-foot-two and weight of 205 pounds, Konstanty could not throw a good fastball. He relied on his control and on a pitch he called "the palm ball." These two things were good enough for him to win at Toronto. But he did not think they would be sufficient in the major leagues.

Eddie Sawyer, the manager of the Phillies, disagreed. Sawyer had managed at Toronto in 1947. He had used Konstanty in relief and thought the older pitcher could be just as effective in the majors.

"I have never seen him get hit real hard," Sawyer said. "He is murder to good hitters. He is also the only pitcher I ever saw who pitches better when he is worn out." For some unknown reason Konstanty's pitches broke more sharply when he was tired. Sawyer finally convinced the Phillies that Konstanty would help.

On September 3, 1948, there was a brief story in the Philadelphia newspapers: "The Phillies today purchased Casimir James (Jim) Konstanty from Toronto of the International League. He is a 31-year-old right-hander who wears glasses. He had a 10–10 record in 162 innings at Toronto. He previously played for . . ."

The story did not excite baseball fans in Philadelphia. More exciting things were happening in 1948.

Konstanty (right) poses with Phils manager Eddie Sawyer who brought him up from the minors at the age of 31.

The Phillies were finishing sixth, about normal for them. But they had built a young team that year with rookies such as Curt Simmons, Robin Roberts and Richie Ashburn. Why pay much attention to a 31-year-old pitcher who had already failed twice in the majors?

Nobody paid much attention to Konstanty late in September 1948. He pitched ten innings for the

Phillies and gave up only one run. But people were already looking ahead to 1949.

Konstanty looked bad during 1949 spring training and was almost cut from the squad. But he pitched a few good innings in exhibition games on the way to Philadelphia after training. Sawyer kept him because he knew that his young pitchers would need help in the late innings, and he intended to use Konstanty frequently.

Relief pitchers were still a rarity in 1949. The Yankees had produced some great ones but few teams had two or three men trained to pitch relief, as they do today. Konstanty was a pioneer in the "art" of relief pitching.

"I guess it's an art," he said. "At least they tell me it is. But I never feel that it's much more than just being able to pitch."

He was not resigned to being a relief pitcher, either. "Not on your life," he said. "If I can master a curve ball, I think I can start. Starters, just like home-run hitters, get the money. The rest of us get the leavings."

Konstanty would get into one game out of three. But every day was a work day for him. "I can feel it coming," he said. "I always turn to the bullpen coach and tell him to answer the telephone from the bench. He starts to tell me the phone isn't ringing. But, sure enough, she goes off."

After the phone rang, the big man with number 35 on the back of his pinstriped uniform would get up and start throwing. Even if he didn't get into the game, he would worry the opposing hitters. They were having a difficult time with him. His pitch would float toward home plate, seeming incredibly slow. But when it arrived at the plate, the ball would always be somewhere the batter couldn't quite reach. It would suddenly dip or bend and the batter would beat it down into the dirt. Konstanty was especially good at getting batters to ground into double plays. It was even better than striking them out.

In mid-August the Phillies won seven of eight games. Konstanty saved four of them. The young Phillies improved late in the season and the club spurted to third place, their highest finish since 1917, when they had finished second. Konstanty was one big reason for the high finish. He worked in 53 games, had a 9–5 record and an earned-run average of 3.25.

In 1950 the Phillies were nicknamed "The Whiz Kids." Great things were expected from them. Besides Roberts, Simmons and Ashburn, there were Del Ennis, Dick Sisler, Puddin' Head Jones, Granny Hamner and Andy Seminick—all fine young players.

Most of these men were in the early twenties. Konstanty, now 33, was one of the oldest men on the team. "Jim rarely cuts up with the players in the dressing room," one reporter wrote. "He resembles a school teacher more than a big-league pitcher. . . ."

In fact he was a school teacher in the off season and he acted the part. He was strict about training. He didn't drink, smoke or stay out late. His idea of a good time was to sit in his hotel room and read a book.

Before every game Jim took strenuous exercise. He ran six 100-yard sprints and took deep-breathing exercises between each sprint. He would chase fungoes, take infield practice with the second infield or just throw the ball to loosen up his arm.

In 1950 he worked almost every other day. The fans knew it was the seventh inning when they saw number 35 stand up in the Phils bullpen and start warming up. Konstanty and the Whiz Kids put the Phillies into first place early in the season. It looked like their year. Until mid-August they seemed to be headed for a pennant. Then Curt Simmons, one of their starting pitchers, was called into the service. Suddenly Konstanty slumped and so did the Phillies. The Brooklyn Dodgers, who had stayed close behind the Phillies, started to move. People began to wonder whether the 33-year-old pitcher and the Whiz Kids had run out of steam a month too soon.

One day the reporters were writing their stories after a game. They were sitting in the pressbox, just under the roof at Shibe Park, where the Phillies played their home games. The field was deserted. Then they noticed activity in the Phillie bullpen. One reporter trained his binoculars on the bullpen and saw Jim Konstanty throwing to a man nobody recognized. The man wore street shoes and slacks and had draped his white shirt over the grandstand railing.

The reporters rushed out to the bullpen and asked Konstanty what was happening.

"This is Andy Skinner," Konstanty said. "He's a friend of mine from Worcester, New York."

Konstanty explained that Skinner caught his pitching every winter in the high-school gym at home. He said Skinner understood his pitching better than anybody in the world.

"In checking the records, I noticed that I had only one strikeout in eighteen innings," Konstanty said. "I came to the conclusion that my slider wasn't breaking right. I called Andy at Worcester and he drove down here overnight, three hundred miles. He was here before today's game. I paid for his gasoline. He wouldn't let me pay any more. But I'll tell you this: if Andy Skinner asked for twenty-five per cent of my salary, I'd give it to him. I owe an awful lot to this man."

The reporters asked if Skinner had ever played baseball.

"No, but he understands my pitching," Konstanty

said. "That's enough."

What did Skinner do for a living?

"I'm an undertaker," Skinner said.

The reporters enjoyed writing about the undertaker who was bringing Jim Konstanty's slider back to life. But the rest of the league didn't think it was funny. Konstanty's pitching perked up again and Sawyer was able to use him regularly again.

The Dodgers chased the Phils into the last day of the season. The Philadelphia team led by one game, but they had to play the Dodgers at Brooklyn's Ebbets Field. Robin Roberts pitched for the Phillies. He almost lost in the ninth but Richie Ashburn, the Phillies' center fielder, threw out a Dodger runner at home plate to send the game into extra innings. Then Dick Sisler slammed a homer in the tenth and the Phillies had won their first pennant in 35 years.

But Roberts was exhausted from the final game. And Sawyer needed somebody to pitch the opening game of the World Series against the New York Yankees. His announcement was a big surprise.

"My starting pitcher is Jim Konstanty," Sawyer said. "With Roberts not ready, Konstanty is the best pitcher I've got. He's gone nine innings in relief in other games. There's no reason why he can't go nine innings as a starter. Besides, the Yankees are fastball hitters. Everybody knows Jim doesn't have a fastball."

Konstanty had pitched in 74 games during the season—a major league record. He won 16 and saved 30 others. He lost only 7. His earned-run average was a low 2.66. But he had not started a game all year. Now he got a chance at one of the biggest games of the year—the World Series opener.

The game was scoreless after three innings. Then the Yankees' Bobby Brown, leading off the fourth, swung at an inside pitch and tapped the ball with the handle of his bat. The ball skittered down the third baseline into left field for a double.

Konstanty wiped his glasses, hitched his belt and went to work against the dangerous Hank Bauer. Bauer slammed a fly to deep center field. By the time Ashburn caught it and returned it to the infield, Brown had tagged up and gone to third. Then Jerry Coleman tapped a fly ball to left field. Brown tagged up again and scored. The Yankees led, 1–0.

Neither team scored again. Konstanty pitched a four-hitter, but the Yankees' Vic Raschi pitched a two-hitter. And the Yankees won the first game of the World Series, 1–0.

"Konstanty is a great pitcher," the Yankee manager, Casey Stengel, raved. "Sawyer certainly knew what he was doing when he started him. He was no gamble. If I had him, I would have started him, too."

The only relief pitcher ever to become MVP, Konstanty shows the pitch that brought the Phillies a pennant—the palm ball.

"He showed us something today," said the Yankees' Joe DiMaggio. "He's a fine pitcher."

Konstanty pitched in the third and fourth games in relief. He gave up only four runs in 15 innings. But the Yankees won the Series in four straight games.

"I didn't believe they could beat us four straight," Konstanty said. "We were beaten but we weren't outclassed."

A month later Konstanty was given 286 points out of a possible 336 in the voting for the Most Valuable Player award. He was the first relief pitcher in history to win the award.

"It's something a pitcher can't win alone," Konstanty said. "I never could have won it without help from the rest of the team. It's something you always work for and never expect. I'm very happy and delighted."

Konstanty looked forward to many more years of relief pitching. "I used to want to be a starter," he said. "But I think that Joe Page and I have changed things. Now you can make money as a relief pitcher. People know how much a good reliever is worth."

Unfortunately he wasn't such a good relief pitcher after 1950. He had only a 4–11 record in 1951 and the Phillies fell to fifth place. Some people said that

Jim receives the MVP award from Baseball Commissioner Ford Frick.

Konstanty was trying too hard to throw a fastball—something he hadn't been able to do for ten years. Others criticized him for listening to his friend Andy Skinner, who made several trips to Philadelphia but couldn't straighten him out as he had in 1950. There were rumors that the Phillie coaches resented Skinner's extra coaching.

Konstanty pitched in only 58 games in 1951. In 1952 he pitched only 42 times. In 1953 he was tried as a starter and pitched 171 innings, the most he ever pitched in the majors. But his days were numbered in Philadelphia.

The Yankees' Casey Stengel, who had never forgotten Konstanty's great performances in the 1950 World Series, bought Konstanty from the Phillies in August, 1954. Konstanty had a few good years with the Yanks. Then he returned to his home in upstate New York to teach and run a sporting-goods store.

In 1963 the Phillies brought back all the old Whiz Kids to play a brief old-timers game. The old-timers were trying to recapture their lost youth, and the fans in the grandstand were chuckling. Suddenly there was a noise overhead. The fans looked up and saw a helicopter. It landed on the pitcher's mound. A husky man with number 35 on his back stepped out of the helicopter.

The Philadelphia fans cheered for several minutes. They had seen Jim Konstanty arrive on the pitcher's mound many, many times before. But this was the first time he had ever arrived by air.

9
YOGI BERRA

Most Valuable Player, American League,
1951, 1954, 1955

People always laughed at Larry Berra's appearance,
even when he was a youth in St. Louis. He was
chunky and plain-looking and his ears seemed to flap
out too far from his head.

One day when he was eleven, he and his friends
went to a movie about India. One of the characters
in the movie was a yogi, a Hindu wise man. When
the gang left the movie and took one look at Lawrence
Peter Berra in broad daylight, they shouted, "That's
you. You look like a yogi!"

So he was Yogi from then on. He dropped out of school after the ninth grade and held a number of different jobs. Finally in 1943 the New York Yankees gave him a bonus of only $500 and sent him to the minor leagues.

People still laughed at Yogi when he reported to the minor league team in Norfolk, Virginia. He was only seventeen years old and he was usually hungry because he couldn't get enough to eat on a minor league salary. He didn't hit well at first and the remarks of the fans about his performance and his appearance hurt him. Fortunately he had a manager who understood what was happening. "Look," said Shaky Kane, "this is gonna happen. More to you than to others. And in language worse than you're hearing. You gotta learn not to get mad."

It was a good lesson and Yogi never forgot it. The next year he went into the Navy. The United States was fighting in World War II, and he saw some duty in the Atlantic. Then he was assigned to a naval base in New London, Connecticut, to help in the recreation program. The officer in charge of recreation was a former major league ballplayer named Jimmy Gleeson. He took one look at the chunky sailor and said, "What do you do?"

"I'm a ballplayer," Yogi said.

"You look more like a wrestler," Gleeson muttered.

But Yogi convinced him that he really was a ball-player. Gleeson put him on the base team and Yogi started to hit. Mel Ott, the manager of the New York Giants, happened to see Yogi hit one day. Ott tried to get the Giants to buy Yogi from the Yankees. But the Yankees refused to sell him, figuring that if Berra was worth something to the Giants, he should be worth something to them, too.

Berra made his first visit to Yankee Stadium in an unusual way. During the fall of 1945 he helped out as equipment manager of the New London football team. New London played a game in Yankee Stadium, and Berra went down with the team.

The New London team dressed in the Yankee clubhouse. Berra was in paradise. He had never seen a clubhouse like it. The lockers were as big as three telephone booths. There was a thick rug on the floor. Everything was clean and neat and comfortable.

"This is some clubhouse," Yogi said to the Yankee clubhouse man, Pete Previte. "I'm really gonna like this when I get up here."

"What do you mean, when you get up here?" Previte sniffed. Previte had been clubhouse man for the great Yankee teams. He couldn't imagine this chunky sailor using the same clubhouse as Joe Di-Maggio and the other Yankee stars.

"I belong to the Yankees," Berra insisted. "I'm

gonna play for Newark next year. But I'll be up here in two years."

Previte nodded. He'd believe it when he saw it.

Berra went to Newark in 1946 and batted .314. The Yankees were so impressed that they brought him across the Hudson River to New York for the last two weeks of the Yankee season.

Not even the formidable, pin-striped Yankee uniform made Berra look like Joe DiMaggio. Yogi was still short, chunky and homely. But he batted .364 during the last week of the 1946 season.

The laughs continued to come. In the spring of 1947 Berra was assigned to room with Bobby Brown, an intelligent young third baseman, who was studying to be a doctor. Reporters imagined a scene in which Brown was reading a complicated medical book and Berra, the drop-out, was reading a comic book. Actually Brown and Berra understood each other and became good friends.

One reporter began to call Berra "The Ape." Other teams soon picked up the title. When Berra came to bat, the opposing team sometimes made apelike noises from the dugout. One player hung from the roof of the dugout and imitated a monkey.

Yogi even looked funny in the batter's box. He shuffled, looking almost sheepish, into the batter's box. Most good hitters stride up to bat like a gunfighter striding down the center of Main Street at high noon. Yogi ducked his head, swung his bat aimlessly a few times, and twitched his legs. He hunched himself up like a gnome.

But there the laughter ended. Berra could hit. He had strong wrists and a good eye and he could get his bat on any pitch. The pitchers tried to take advantage of him by giving him bad pitches. He looked like the kind of eager rookie who would swing at anything. He was—but with a difference. He could hit anything.

"You shouldn't have any trouble with Berra," somebody told Hal Newhouser of Detroit, one of the league's best pitchers. "He's strictly a bad-ball hitter."

"Yeah," Newhouser grumbled. "But I defy anybody to throw him a good pitch."

Berra was at his strongest late in the game. There was something about a close game, with runners on base, that made Berra extra dangerous. He would swat a few line drives foul into the right-field stands. The crowd would roar at each foul. The pitcher would grow tired and desperate. Then Berra would break up the game with a base hit. He was a "money player," meaning that he played his best when the chips were down.

Yogi made rapid progress. The Yankees hired their former catching star, Bill Dickey, to coach Berra.

Berra looked funny in the batter's box but when the chips were down, he nearly always came through with a hit.

Dickey made him into a respectable catcher, although Yogi had some bad moments with his glove. In his first year he batted .280 and established himself as an important Yankee. In 1950 Yogi even passed the great Joe DiMaggio in one important category. DiMaggio drove in 122 runs during the year; Berra drove in 124.

The Yankees had a critical season in 1951. DiMaggio was playing his last season and Mickey Mantle, his successor, was a raw rookie. Some of the other veterans were getting old. But the man who held the Yankees together and led them to the pennant was Lawrence Peter Berra.

Yogi was so important that manager Casey Stengel called him "my assistant manager." Stengel claimed that the Yankees didn't need to keep records on other teams because Berra remembered everything. This was Stengel's way of warning the reporters and opponents not to make too many jokes about Yogi. "Mr. Berra can get to the park without a map," Stengel said.

It was a good thing that Yogi did get to the park. The Yankees needed him. One night the Boston Red Sox brought in left-hander Mickey McDermott to protect a lead. The bases were loaded and Berra was up. McDermott decided to waste a pitch. He threw it over Yogi's head. Yogi swatted at the ball and drilled it into the right-field seats for a grand-slam

Yogi strains for a foul ball off Ted Williams' bat. He dropped it and almost cost the pitcher a no-hitter.

home run. The Yankees won the game.

On September 28 the Yankees were in Boston for a double-header. Allie Reynolds, the Yankee ace, pitched in the first game. He had pitched a no-hitter against Cleveland in July, and now he needed to get only one more batter out for another no-hitter.

But the next man up for Boston was Ted Williams, one of the greatest hitters in baseball. Reynolds forced Williams to loft a pop foul behind home plate. Yogi drifted back, tossed away his mask, stuck up his glove—and dropped the ball!

"I think it was my worst moment in baseball," Berra said later.

Reynolds got Williams to hit another pop-up to Berra. "Son of a gun, what if I drop this one, too?" Yogi muttered to himself as he waited under the ball. But he didn't drop this one and Reynolds had his second no-hitter. Then the Yankees won the second game and wrapped up their pennant.

Yogi played in 141 games in 1951, more than Di-Maggio or Mantle. He drove in 88 runs and batted .294. The Yankees went on to win the World Series. And Yogi Berra went on to win the Most Valuable Player award.

"That really made me feel good," he said. "I could hardly believe I'd won the award because so many great hitters have won it before me—DiMaggio, Williams, Lou Boudreau, Phil Rizzuto. . . . It made me very proud."

Yogi wasn't through. He received a special honor in 1954 when he was named Most Valuable Player again. It might have seemed more logical for a member of the pennant-winning Cleveland Indians to get the award. But Yogi's total of 125 runs batted in earned him the award once again.

He won it a third time in 1955. Nobody has ever won the award more than three times. And only six men—DiMaggio, Mantle, Foxx, Musial, Campanella and Berra—have won it three times.

Yogi remained a valuable Yankee after 1955. He shared the catching job with Elston Howard (who was Most Valuable Player in 1963) and sometimes Yogi took a turn in the outfield. In 1963 the Yankees made him a player–coach. He batted .293 and the Yankees won another pennant. He played 17 seasons for them and they won 14 pennants.

In 1964 the Yankees provided a big surprise. They made Yogi manager of the club. He gave up playing, but his winning touch didn't leave him. The Yankees rallied to win 99 games and the pennant. Then they lost the World Series in seven games to St. Louis.

The day after the Series ended, the Yankee front office had another surprise. They fired Yogi "for the good of the team." Most people knew that Yogi was not an inspirational manager. He did not have the strength of Ralph Houk, who had managed the Yankees during the previous season, or the brilliance of Casey Stengel, for whom Yogi had played on nearly a dozen pennant-winning teams. But he had still won a pennant in his only year as manager. Many Yankee fans were puzzled by the sudden change.

Yogi did not complain. He had learned long ago,

Yogi has a bad day as Yankee manager.

back in 1943 under Shaky Kane at Norfolk, to shrug off misfortune. Besides, he had a happy family and a good business outside baseball.

His old boss, Casey Stengel, who was then managing the New York Mets, hadn't forgotten his "assistant manager." Casey hired Yogi as a coach with the Mets in 1965. Yogi even caught a few games. But Yogi told Casey "I can't do it any more" and retired to the coaching line. Yogi still looked funny, wearing his orange-and-blue number 8 uniform. But Casey was still warning the world not to forget about Yogi.

"Don't laugh at Mr. Berra," Casey said. "That other team [the Yankees] may have fired him. But Mr. Berra has never failed yet."

10
ERNIE BANKS

Most Valuable Player, National League, 1958, 1959

I

The Chicago Cubs once were one of baseball's best teams. They won ten pennants between 1900 and 1945. And even today they have the third best record in the National League since 1900.

But by the time Ernie Banks arrived in 1953, the Cubs were in trouble. They had won their last pennant in 1945. In 1946 they slipped to third place; the following year they fell into the second division where they remained in 1953. In addition, Chicago's Wrigley Field remained the only park in the major leagues

118

without night baseball. Phillip K. Wrigley, the Cubs' owner, didn't want to disturb the people who live around Wrigley Field, so he had never had lights installed at the stadium.

The fans didn't have a good team and they didn't have night baseball. But they did always manage to have a good home run hitter.

There were always homers soaring out of Wrigley Field, some days six or eight of them. One reason for the homers was the famous Chicago wind. The wind off Lake Michigan, a mile east of Wrigley Field, usually blows toward the outfield. In the spring the field is like a wind tunnel. But the better Cub sluggers didn't need much help anyway.

In 1953 the Cubs purchased Ernie Banks from the Kansas City Monarchs, one of the best teams in the Negro leagues. Ernie was a tremendous hero in Kansas City. He didn't look like a slugger because he was slender at six-foot-one and 180 pounds. His arms and shoulders were thin but his wrists were strong. "You grab hold of him," said the Cub manager, Bob Scheffing, "and it's like grabbing hold of steel."

The Cubs brought the 22-year-old shortstop in for the last ten games of the 1953 season. Banks batted .314 and slugged two homers. The next spring he was the regular shortstop. He batted .275, and hit nineteen homers. But Hank Sauer and Ralph Kiner were still the slugging stars of the Windy City.

Late in the 1954 season an important thing happened to Ernie. The Cubs were playing the New York Giants and Banks was talking with the Giant players. Banks was already one of the leading chatterers in the major leagues. Although there is a baseball rule against players "fraternizing" before games, most players are friendly with their opponents, particularly Ernie Banks.

Banks was chatting with Monte Irvin, the Giants' leading run-producer. He picked up Irvin's bat and swung it a couple of times.

"It felt real good," Banks said. "It weighed only 31 ounces. I had been using a heavier bat. It had a thin handle. I could hit an outside pitch. It was easy to swing. It whipped better than a heavier bat, particularly for a wrist hitter like me. . . ."

A scientist later estimated that Banks' swing was increased 20 miles per hour by using a bat two or three ounces lighter. Ernie stocked up on 31-ounce bats for the 1955 season and the home runs started to fly. He drove in 117 runs and slammed 44 homers that year, more than Sauer or Kiner ever hit in Chicago. The 44 homers set a major league record for shortstops.

On September 19 Banks was batting against the St. Louis Cardinals. Lindy McDaniel had loaded the

Banks knows more than one way to get on base. Here he brings his bat around to bunt.

bases. Banks drilled a homer into Waveland Avenue, behind left field. It was his fifth grand-slam homer of the season—another major-league record.

People were starting to call him the best shortstop in the league. "For a good shortstop, you sacrifice hitting," said Frank Lane, the envious general manager of the White Sox. "Leo Durocher and Marty Marion were both weak hitters. But Banks is a good hitter *and* a good fielder. He can wait until the ball is right up there, then he flicks that 31-ounce bat and—there goes the ball game!"

Banks became the most important player on the team. "Ernie's no holler guy," Scheffing said. "But he's the steadying influence on the team . . . and you never hear him complain about a thing."

That was certainly true. The face Banks turned to the world was always gay. The Cubs could be fifty games out of first place. But Banks would say to his teammates: "We're going to win today. You watch. The Cubbies are making their move." His teammates would smile. It was more pleasant to lose with Ernie around.

Ernie became the biggest hero on the North Side. At practice, he would take his swings, then amble over to the brick wall that separates the field from the stands. The fans would line up and scream for Ernie to give them his autograph. He would sign, sometimes for as long as an hour.

"Who's going to win today?" Ernie would ask.

"The Cubs, the Cubs," the children would shout.

"Now you're talking," Ernie would say.

The Cubs didn't win very often. But the fans had somebody to root for. Banks hit only 28 homers in 1956. Then he hit 43 in 1957. The fans continued to come to the ball park although the Cubs never finished higher than sixth out of the eight teams then in the league.

In 1958 the pitchers decided to stop Banks. Jack Sanford of the Phillies seemed to aim more at Banks than at the plate. There was a stretch when Ernie was hit by a pitch in four straight games. In each game, on the very next time up, he hit a homer.

But Ernie never got mad and he never tried anything violent against the pitchers. He just got up and swung. "I can't recall Ernie ever losing his temper," said George Altman, later a teammate of Ernie's. "He's always the same, smiling and happy."

Ernie smiled a lot in 1958. He raised his record for homers by a shortstop to 47 and drove in 129 runs. The Cubs actually moved into a tie for fifth place with the Cardinals.

The baseball writers recognized achievement when they saw it. Ernie's total of 129 runs batted in, for instance, was more remarkable with the Cubs than it

Jumping over Cincinnati's Roy McMillan, Banks completes a double play.

would have been had he played for a strong-hitting team. Since fewer of Ernie's teammates got on base, he probably had fewer chances than men on other teams to drive runs in. The writers voted Banks the National League's Most Valuable Player for 1958. Only Hank Sauer, back in 1952, had ever won a Most Valuable Player award on a second division team.

Ernie won the award again in 1959. This time he slugged 45 homers and drove in 143 runs, the most he had ever driven in during a season. And the Cubs shared fifth place with the Reds. Ernie was the first National Leaguer to win the MVP award two years in a row. He set two other records in 1959. He made fewer errors, 12, than any shortstop had ever made in one season and he had the highest fielding percentage of any shortstop in history, .985.

Many observers believe that Ernie was not a great

shortstop despite his fine fielding record. He never had a strong arm so he played in close. Many troublesome grounders got past him before he even had a chance to touch them. Nevertheless he was a good, reliable fielder.

In 1960 Banks hit 41 homers and drove in 117 runs. But the Cubs fell back to seventh place. In 1961 the Cubs moved him from shortstop to left field. It was a terrific blow to him. They said his arm, his eyesight and his range had all diminished. Ernie himself announced that he had asked to play left field, but he was unable to hide his disappointment. He hit only 29 home runs that year.

In 1962 Ernie was moved again, this time to first base. There he would be closer to the action and could chatter with the other players again. He perked up and hit 37 homers. At 31 years of age he seemed to have a new career.

Then in 1963 Ernie felt weak and miserable most of the season. He hit only 18 homers and people said he was all washed up. It was the worst possible year for Ernie to falter. The Cubs had gotten off to a good start, and they finally managed to sneak into first place one night in June. It was the first time Banks had ever been in first place in the major leagues. But they slipped right out of first again, as Ernie continued to slump, and finished seventh.

"I feel bad for Ernie," said the Cubs' head coach, Bob Kennedy. "I know he feels worse than anybody."

Later the doctors found that Ernie had been suffering from a mild case of the mumps, which he had caught from his children. Ernie had feared he was suffering from something much worse. He perked up in 1964 and 1965, hitting 23 and 28 homers, but he never again approached his Most Valuable Player totals.

Ernie was not even the best ballplayer on the Cubs anymore. Billy Williams was one of the leading hitters in the league. And third baseman Ron Santo was the hustling leader of the team, something Banks had never quite become. But Ernie was still special at Wrigley Field. The fans and reporters still clustered around him. They loved to hear his old, old story.

"Look at this beautiful ball park," he would say, waving his hand. "Look at the ivy on the walls. Look at that scoreboard. Read what it says: night baseball, night baseball. Only one afternoon game in the major leagues today, folks.

"Tonight on the six o'clock news, the man will announce that the Cubbies win another one. That's the only way to play. In the daytime. In the sunlight. It's the natural way. They play the World Series in the day time, don't they? Wait until we're

Returning to the infield, Banks developed into a good first baseman. Here he puts out the Mets' Ron Swoboda.

in the World Series. This is the year. I feel it. We're going to win the Series. . . ."

Ernie has been promising a World Series in Wrigley Field since 1953, but the Cubs haven't even left the second division. Ernie may not believe what he says and perhaps his career with a losing team makes him sad. But he keeps on laughing.

Many Cub fans feel that the Cubs can lose all the time and it can rain every other day. But as long as Ernie Banks is around, it will always be a lovely day for a ball game.

11
MICKEY MANTLE

Most Valuable Player, American League,
1956, 1957, 1962

Casey Stengel could hardly believe his eyes: there in a New York Yankee uniform was the super ball-player he had been searching for. Stengel watched the blond, broad-shouldered young man run from home plate to first base in 3.1 seconds, one of the fastest times in baseball history. Then he watched him swat 500-foot homers in batting practice and slash line drives left-handed and right-handed. It was the spring of 1951 and the new wonder was just nineteen years old. He had made 55 errors at

128

shortstop in Class C ball during the previous year. But Stengel saw greatness in him, envisioning one of the most powerful outfielders ever to wear a Yankee uniform. The young man's name—Mickey Mantle.

Casey knew that Mantle should play another year in the minor leagues but he could not bear to part with him. On his own time the old manager taught the young man how to play right field. In the back of his mind he knew that Mantle would replace Joe DiMaggio in center field within a year.

When the Yankees went north to open the season, Casey escorted Mantle to right field during practices. "He's never seen concrete before," Stengel said. Mantle had played only in rickety wooden minor league parks. But there was more to the major leagues than concrete and steel stadiums. Major league pitchers handcuffed Mantle during the first half of the season. Stengel finally sent him to the Yanks' Kansas City farm team in July.

Mickey was crushed. He had always been a temperamental boy and this was a big blow to him. Then his father, Mutt Mantle, a zinc miner in Commerce, Oklahoma, came to visit Mickey in Kansas City.

Mutt had always wanted to play professional baseball, but he had never been able to leave his

Mickey consults with manager Casey Stengel who brought Mickey up to the majors.

job at the mines. So he had played semiprofessional baseball and encouraged his son to become a ball-player.

"It takes guts, not moaning, to bounce back," Mutt Mantle told his son. His words stung Mickey and soon he had snapped back and was hitting .361 for Kansas City. He was called back to the Yankees in August.

It looked as if only happy days were ahead for the Mantles. The Yankees won the pennant and Mickey raised his average to .267. He opened the

World Series in right field, next to the great DiMaggio in center field. In the second game Mantle was chasing a fly ball in the outfield. Suddenly he pitched forward on his face. By the time his teammates got to him, Mantle was in very great pain. He had caught his foot in a drainage pipe that had been left open by mistake, and had torn up his knee. His teammates carried him off the field.

The next day, Mutt Mantle accompanied his injured son to the hospital and stayed there with him. Mickey's father was suffering from Hodgkin's Disease and had only a few months to live. He lived to see his son become a major-league player, but he missed the great years that followed.

Mantle's knee healed and, beginning in 1952, he replaced Joe DiMaggio in center field. In the following years he had many great moments. He hit a 565-foot homer in Washington's Griffith Stadium. Twice he missed by inches becoming the first player ever to hit a fair ball over the roof of Yankee Stadium. He became the new Yankee star, just as Stengel had predicted.

But for every great moment there was also pain. Mantle had come into baseball suffering from an arrested case of osteomyelitis, a bone disease. The knee he injured in 1951 required an operation and was rarely sound after that. He suffered from

Mantle shows his batting form both left- and right-handed.

assorted bone and muscle aches.

The only season when Mantle felt he was completely healthy was 1956. He won baseball's Triple Crown that year, leading the American League in batting average (.353), home runs (52) and runs batted in (130). The Yankees won the pennant and the World Series. And Mickey Mantle was voted Most Valuable Player. In 1957 he suffered from shin splints and missed ten games. But he hit .365, his highest average ever, and the Yankees won another pennant. Once again Mantle was voted Most Valuable Player.

His teammates treated him like a Most Valuable Player. They knew he was a great clutch hitter, a fine outfielder, a team player in spite of his struggles with injuries. "I never had goose pimples in my life until the day I saw Mickey Mantle limp up to home plate and hit a home run," said his teammate Bobby Richardson.

When Mantle dressed for a game, the other Yankees saw him wrap yards of tape around his knees. They saw him struggle to climb stairs, pulling himself along with his powerful arms. They heard him gasp with pain when he swung and missed. Even the other team heard those gasps.

"I see him swing sometimes," said Carl Yastrzemski, a fine Boston outfielder. "Even from the outfield you can see the leg buckle under him and when he winces in pain, I wince too. It's like your kid is in pain and you can feel the pain yourself. That's the way ballplayers feel about Mantle."

Mantle inspired the Yankees with his home runs and with his hillbilly sense of humor. He would swagger up and down the dugout or the aisle of an airplane, imitating a tough cowboy or making fun of himself in a recent game.

Yankee veterans remember arriving in Milwaukee for the sixth game of the 1958 World Series. They had lost the 1957 Series to the Braves and now they were behind three games to two. They were very serious and quiet on the darkened team bus. Then Mantle stood up and announced in a deep, mock-serious voice, "This is it, fellows." The players exploded with laughter at his gag. They relaxed and went on to win the next two games and the Series. They all depended on him.

Misfortune struck again on the night of May 18, 1962. The Yankees were losing, 4–3, to the Minnesota Twins with two outs in the ninth inning. There was a runner on second. Mantle slammed a ground ball to the shortstop. He hit the ball so hard that shortstop Zoilo Versalles was knocked back a step by the impact. Mantle sensed that the play at first would be very close. He hurtled toward first base

Mantle sprawls on the baseline after tearing a thigh muscle trying to beat a throw to first base. Twins first baseman Vic Power is the first to the scene.

as Versalles regained his balance and fired the ball.

Suddenly the Yankee star bounded through the air like an animal that has been shot. He fell to the ground, writhing in pain, still fifteen feet short of the base. He was out, of course, and the game was over. But the fans stayed to see what had stricken the great star. The Yankees surrounded Mantle, who was gripping his right thigh and moaning. But when a stretcher was summoned, Mantle refused to ride it. He hobbled off the field supported by teammates.

The Yankee clubhouse was ghostly. The players just sat in front of their lockers, slowly removing their uniforms. They wouldn't leave until they found out what had happened to Mantle. The team trainer and the physician were attending him in the trainer's room.

An hour later Mantle hobbled on crutches into the locker room. He was fully dressed and his face was pasty white. He waved at them all and said in his cowboy drawl: "See y'all." But they knew they wouldn't be seeing him soon.

Mantle had torn his thigh muscle. He had also bruised a ligament in his left knee while falling. He did not return for thirty games, and the Yankees lost half of them. They couldn't seem to get fired up without Mantle.

It was late June and the Yankees were in Cleveland when Mantle limped into the clubhouse and pulled on his uniform again. The players tried to act nonchalant about it but they couldn't. They were overjoyed to see him back. Just having him around was good. He played catch before the game, daring anybody to catch his knuckleball. The players laughed at his antics; they knew they were going to be all right again.

Mantle didn't play the first day. The next afternoon the Yankees were a run behind in the eighth inning. They put two men on base. The Yankee manager, Ralph Houk, looked at Mantle, who nodded and reached for his bat. With every Yankee and every fan staring at him, Mantle limped up to home plate.

He swung and smashed a three-run homer. Later he described the moment as "my biggest kick of the season."

The Yankees lost all four games in Cleveland that weekend and fell out of first place. But on the way home they acted as if they had just won the World Series. Later in the week Mantle played his first full game. At the end of the week the Yankees were back on top.

In September Mantle hit two tremendous homers to beat Washington. Afterwards he was asked who should be Most Valuable Player. "Bobby Richardson," Mantle said. "He's played with injuries and he's batting .300."

Richardson pointed at all the Yankees who were congratulating Mantle for the two homers. "I think what happened tonight pretty much summed up the feeling on this club," Richardson said.

With Mantle batting .450 during the last month of the season, the Yankees won the pennant by five games. Then they beat San Francisco in seven games of the World Series. During the Series celebration Mantle strutted around with a cardboard medal pinned to his suit. His best friend, pitcher Whitey Ford, had constructed it. "It's for batting .120 in the World Series," said Ford.

"It's for the most guts in the Series," Mantle

corrected Ford. "I got it just for showing up every day." This was his kind of humor—strong and usually directed at himself.

Still laughing the Yankees departed for their homes all around the country. Mantle was playing golf near his home in Dallas, Texas, two weeks later when somebody placed a telephone call to him on the golf course. It was to announce that Mantle was Most Valuable Player for the third time.

"I thought it would be Bobby Richardson," Mantle said.

It might have been. Richardson batted .302, played second base very well and was admired by his teammates for his hustle and personality. But there was nobody like Mickey Mantle on the Yankee roster. He played 123 games in 1962, despite his injuries. He batted .321, drove in 89 runs, hit 30 homers and was even more valuable than the statistics showed.

It took the fans longer to appreciate Mantle than it took the players. Yankee fans hadn't needed new heroes when Mantle arrived. And they didn't like Mantle for a long time. They saw him toss his batting helmet away or pound his bat into the ground when he struck out. They saw him sulk in the outfield when he was playing badly. They booed him. The fans didn't understand that Mantle was still a young country boy. He had spent very little time

Mickey thrilled the fans with his fielding too. Here he chases a fly to deepest center field.

in major league ball parks and didn't understand what fans expected from their heroes.

Spectators expect their heroes to notice them, to smile, to wave once in a while. Mantle didn't. Thousands of fans would mill around Mantle at the ball park. Sometimes their noise and roughness upset him so much that he bolted through a crowd, spilling youngsters in his wake. He never meant to be unkind. But for ten years the boos were almost as thick as the cheers in New York.

"When I first broke in, the fans got down on me and I got down on myself," Mantle recalls. "I was so new, I didn't know what to expect. For a few years the fans and I had a little go-around. But it all changed."

Mantle remembers the day he knew things had changed. It happened in 1963, the year after he was MVP. He broke his foot in June and wasn't ready to play again until August. He still couldn't play in the outfield but he was ready to pinch-hit. The Yankees were trailing the Orioles, 10–9, in Yankee Stadium on a Sunday afternoon. It was the bottom of the seventh inning; there were two outs and nobody was on. Manager Houk nodded at Mantle. Mantle nodded back.

All 38,555 fans roared with approval when they saw number 7 come out of the dugout and walk stiff-legged up to home plate.

"The ovation actually chilled me," Mantle said. "I was shaking. I could feel the bumps rising on my arms. When I got out of the dugout, I said to myself, 'Be sure to swing. Don't stand there and take three pitches.'"

Mantle swung at the second pitch. He drove it 390 feet over the left-center field fence. He trotted around the bases slowly, favoring his sore leg. The fans stood up and applauded. The ovation has been called one of the greatest ever in Yankee Stadium.

"Even if I was deaf, I could have heard them," Mantle said. "They cheered before I even did anything. You have no idea how good that made me feel."

After 1962 injuries kept him out of too many games to be considered for the Most Valuable Player award. The injuries also kept him from becoming the super player Casey Stengel had envisioned back in 1951. But for fifteen years Mantle had been one of baseball's greatest sluggers. Perhaps his biggest achievement was winning over the fans. He became one of New York's biggest sports heroes—for being one of the most valuable players in history, and for being one of the most courageous.

12
MAURY WILLS

Most Valuable Player, National League, 1962

Maury Wills began his baseball career with great enthusiasm. He was a bright-eyed 18-year-old, and he felt he was going to be great. But seven years later his enthusiasm had died. He had not made the major leagues yet, and he doubted he would ever make them. He was playing baseball at Spokane, Washington, just to make a living. But the fun had gone out of baseball.

Wills was not as dedicated as he had been. One day when he was bored with practice, he jumped

into the batting cage and hit left-handed although
he had always been a right-handed hitter.

The manager at Spokane, was Bobby Bragan.
Bragan had never been a very good major league
player, but he had always tried to improve himself.
After watching Wills in the batting cage, he said,
"Why don't you really try hitting left-handed?"

"I'm too old to learn," Wills said. "I'm twenty-five."

"You're never too old," Bragan replied.

Bragan urged the slender infielder to try switch-
hitting. He even volunteered to pitch extra batting
practice. "By batting left-handed against right-
handed pitchers," he explained, "you see the ball
better. You're also a step closer to first base after
you swing."

It took a few weeks of practice but Wills soon saw
the advantages of switch-hitting. He had always
been a fast runner. But when he batted left-handed
he got to first base even faster. He became a better
hitter than ever.

The next year was 1959. The Los Angeles Dodgers
owned the Spokane club but they didn't want Wills
—even with his new switch-hitting. They sold him
to Detroit that spring, but Detroit returned him to
Spokane.

"I guess I should have been disappointed," Wills
said. "But I wasn't. I had finally been given a

To make the majors, Wills had to improve his hitting. Here he smacks one right-handed.

chance and I almost made it. I was sure another chance would come."

The Dodgers, meanwhile, were having shortstop problems. They had always seemed to have a dozen young shortstops while Pee Wee Reese was the irreplaceable Dodger shortstop. But when Reese retired in 1959, all the good shortstops seemed to have vanished. The Dodgers decided to give Wills, who was batting .313 at Spokane, a chance.

The city of Los Angeles did not exactly stage a celebration for Wills. When he arrived on June 2, he was greeted by a sarcastic headline in one of the Los Angeles papers: "MAURY WILLS . . . WHO ARE THEY KIDDING?"

But Wills was determined to make the most of his chance. He batted .260 for the rest of the season, and the Dodgers beat Milwaukee in a play-off to win the pennant. Wills hit .250 and fielded well in the World Series, which the Dodgers also won.

But the following spring Wills was treated like a minor leaguer once again. The regular Dodgers —all the other men who had played in the 1959 World Series—were living in pleasant two-man rooms at the training camp. Wills was assigned to the four-man barracks where the scrubs lived.

The demotion set him off wrong and he played badly during the season. He was hitting below .200 and losing his job day by day. Manager Walter Alston was still starting Wills but he would use a pinch hitter for Maury as early as the third or fourth inning. Then Wills had to take the long walk to the Dodger clubhouse, right past the box seats where the Dodger officials were sitting. He became more and more discouraged. "I was ready to call it quits," he said.

One night he was brooding in the clubhouse after being replaced by a pinch hitter. He was so discouraged that he didn't even remove his uniform. He just sat next to his locker and waited for the game to end. When the other Dodgers trooped in, Wills looked the other way. Then he realized that Dodger coach Pete Reiser was staring at him.

"Pete, what am I going to do?" Wills blurted.

"Don't worry," Reiser said. "Meet me here before practice tomorrow, two hours early, and I'll do what I can."

It was nearly 100 degrees in Los Angeles the next day. The huge Los Angeles Coliseum was like a baking dish. On the floor of the arena the temperature must have been closer to 115.

Reiser and Wills worked until their uniforms were covered with sweat. The coach pitched and hit hundreds of balls at Wills. He made Maury practice everything—swatting the "butcher boy" (a high chopper to the infield), bunting, poking the ball to the opposite field.

"You can't quit," Reiser kept barking. "You have to keep at it. These things don't come overnight."

The practices went on every day for a month. Wills wanted to quit many times but Reiser wouldn't let him. Gradually Maury began to hit and Alston let him play longer and longer. His average went up steadily, reaching .295 by the end of the season. "I'll never forget what Pete Reiser and Bobby Bragan did for me," Maury said later.

Wills hit .289 for the Dodgers in 1961 and made the All-Star team. But his greatest years were still ahead. The next year was a year of change for the Dodgers. They moved from the odd-shaped Coliseum to their new home in Chavez Ravine. Dodger Stadium is surrounded by palm trees and has pastel-colored seats. Another thing it has is distance—the fences are far from home plate. And the air in the stadium seems heavy, "dead air," the ballplayers call it. Home runs come very infrequently.

Some people believed that the stadium was designed for the Dodgers, who had not been a powerful hitting team since they left Brooklyn in 1957. The Dodgers of 1962 had a few sluggers like Frank Howard and Tommy Davis, but almost every other team had more power. The new stadium discouraged teams with power. Men would swing with all their might—and produce 340-foot fly balls. And the Dodgers, with Don Drysdale and Sandy Koufax, usually had the edge in pitching.

Wills saw that one run would be very important in almost every Dodger game. If he could find a way to "steal" one run in every game, he could contribute much to the team. He also noticed that the infield at Dodger Stadium was rock-hard. He practiced slapping ground balls and saw that they skipped through the infield. A man could get a lot of scratch hits if he put the ball in the right place. Then he tested the baselines. Although they were hard, a runner's spikes could get good footing. They felt to Wills like a good running track. A man could steal a lot of bases at Dodger Stadium.

Wills had led the league in stolen bases with 50 in 1960 and 35 in 1961. But nobody was prepared for his antics in 1962. He had practiced six or eight different ways of sliding. He constantly tested pitchers and catchers, daring them to give him a lead off base. His game was different—and it was exciting.

Dodger fans caught on fast. They would shout "go-go-go" every time Wills reached first base. The players sensed the excitement, too.

"Maybe I shouldn't say this," Wills said. "But I think my stolen bases are what stirs this club up. When everything is going along and nothing is happening, I feel I have got to stir things up. When I get on, before you know it, the fans are yelling 'go-go.' The bench comes alive, the manager and the coaches are up, and things start moving for us. I've seen it happen many times."

Unlike some falsely modest players, Wills's ap-

The sight that terrifies opposing teams—Wills heads for second.

proach is: "I have something special to offer. I can help the team in a different way." Sometimes he sounds immodest, almost vain. But as Dizzy Dean said about himself, "If you can do it, it's not bragging."

The Dodgers found out what Wills meant in 1962. He was the first man up and often got on base. He was always ready to run when he got there. Veteran Jim Gilliam, the second man up, was an expert at punching the ball to right field on the hit-and-run and often helped Wills along. The Dodgers always seemed to be circling the bases, forcing the other team to make mistakes. Baseball took on new excitement because of Wills.

Wills had 46 steals in 51 attempts by midseason. More important the Dodgers were in first place. He wanted very much to make the All-Star team in 1962. The game was being played in Washington, D.C., his home town, where dozens of his family and friends could come to watch him. He made the team only as a second choice after Dick Groat of Pittsburgh.

Wills sat on the bench and watched for the first five innings. In the top of the sixth inning manager Fred Hutchinson sent up the great Stan Musial to pinch-hit. There was still no score. "You get a hit for me, Stan," Wills shouted, "and I'll steal a base for you."

Musial ripped a single to center field. Hutchinson turned to tell Wills to run for Musial. But Wills was already racing up the dugout steps and out to first base. The fans cheered—but they were cheering for the 41-year-old Musial, who was leaving the game.

Wills studied Minnesota pitcher Camilo Pascual

as he threw the first pitch. It was a slow overhand
curveball. Wills knew he could steal on that pitch.
Pascual threw again and Wills was off. He got such
a good lead that Minnesota catcher Earl Battey
didn't bother to throw to second.

Then Dick Groat slapped a single. Wills raced
home from second. The National League had a 1–0
lead. Wills then replaced Groat at shortstop and the
National League took a 2–1 lead into the eighth.
The 45,480 fans including President John F. Kennedy,
waited to see what would happen.

Wills singled to open the eighth inning. Then Jim
Davenport of San Francisco ripped a single to left
field. As Wills neared second base, he glanced into
left field. The left fielder was Rocky Colavito of
Detroit, who had one of the strongest throwing arms
in baseball. It seemed like suicide to run on Colavito.
But Wills wheeled right around second base, daring
Rocky to make a throw. As Colavito scooped up the
ball, he saw Wills moving. He threw—but to the
wrong base. Wills scooted right on to third.

The National League had three good hitters, Felipe
Alou, Willie Mays and John Callison, coming up next.
Any one of them was likely to get a hit. But Wills
couldn't wait. When Alou lofted a pop-up behind
first base, Wills watched the first baseman, Leon
Wagner, drift back to make the catch. As soon as

After going from first to third on a short single, Wills slides into home after a routine foul ball in the All-Star game. Catcher John Romano couldn't make the tag and Wills was safe.

the ball touched Wagner's glove, Wills broke for home. It was a risky move, especially with strong hitters coming up. But Wills believed in risk. He slid home safely ahead of Wagner's throw. Now the American League understood what Maury was doing to his National League opponents.

"I never go with a fifty–fifty chance," Wills said after the National League had wrapped up its 3–1 victory. "Fifty-fifty is not enough in my favor. I've eliminated the fear of failing. When I make a move on the bases, I think I'm going to be safe every time. It takes a perfect throw to get me. I know the fielder is thinking he has to rush his throw on me. He can't be as accurate as if he took his time."

After the All-Star break, Wills kept running and sliding until his legs were badly bruised. "Raw hamburger," he said, pointing to the great purple splotches on his legs. Most players wear hip pads to protect themselves from sliding bruises. But Wills felt the pads cut down on his speed.

In the middle of September Maury broke the major league record of 96 stolen bases set by Ty Cobb in 1915. But the Dodgers were in trouble. The Giants were gaining on them. When St. Louis beat the Dodgers three times on the last weekend of the season, the Giants and Dodgers finished in a tie for first. There would be a best-of-three game play-off.

The Giants won the first game, 8–0, and Wills went hitless. The Dodgers won the second game, 8–7. Again Wills didn't make a hit. Now the play-off shifted to Los Angeles for the deciding game.

Maury Wills had four straight singles in the final

game. He stole three bases and scored a run. The Dodgers had a 4–2 lead going into the ninth. But the Giants scored four runs to win the game and the pennant.

The Dodgers were stunned. They had been within three outs of a pennant, but now they were just a second-place team. Many of them sat in the club-house for hours without moving. Wills was as stunned as anybody. He had finished the season with a .299 batting average, 104 stolen bases and 130 runs scored. He had played in every Dodger game all season. Wills was exhausted. His legs were bleeding internally from all his sliding. He had done all he could—but the Dodgers had lost the pennant anyway.

He felt better a month later. The Baseball Writers announced that he was the National League's Most Valuable Player for 1962. "This is the most a player can get." Wills said. "I worked hard, ever since spring training. You only get out of anything what you put into it. If you put in a little extra, sometimes you get something wonderful back."

In 1963 and 1965 Wills helped the Dodgers win world championships. In the 1965 World Series the Dodgers met a team that nearly beat them at their own game. The Minnesota Twins stole bases, played the hit-and-run and forced their opponents into costly

Maury hits the dirt and steals second again.

errors. The lively, daring style of play that Wills had introduced was coming back throughout the majors. With the help of Wills the Dodgers beat the Twins in the seventh game of the series. But it was clear that in addition to helping the Dodgers win pennants, Maury had revolutionized baseball.

13
KEN BOYER

Most Valuable Player, National League, 1964

Ken Boyer was not expected to be the leader of the St. Louis Cardinals when he joined them in 1955. The Cardinals already had the great Stan Musial. Boyer was only supposed to become the National League's best third baseman.

"Ken is the kind of player you wish you had twelve of," said Card manager Fred Hutchinson, "so you could play nine and have three on the bench just to stir things up. He's the kind of guy you dream about. Terrific speed, great arm, brute strength. There's nothing he can't do."

The rookie from the Texas League batted .264 and excited Cardinal fans by stealing 22 bases. He looked too big, standing six-foot two-inches and weighing 205 pounds, to play the infield. But he had quick reflexes and a quick glove. He could play third base or shortstop. When he batted .306 in 1956, the Cardinals thought he was on his way. "Boyer's potential is tremendous," said general manager Frank Lane. "He can be our answer to Mickey Mantle."

Then, because Boyer was such a fine athlete, the Cardinals asked him to shift to center field. But the change of position upset him. He was tried at shortstop again, but he would have preferred third base. Soon his whole game was suffering. "He just doesn't push enough," Hutchinson said. "He has to develop more aggressiveness."

Hutchinson's comments upset Boyer. "I don't think hustle is something you can see all the time," he said. "But I try. I've always had desire."

Boyer seemed to sulk through the 1957 season. He finished with a .265 average and only 62 runs batted in. St. Louis officials decided that he might not reach the heights they had predicted. They were impatient with Boyer because Musial was getting older and the Cardinals had nobody to replace him as star and leader. Boyer had been the candi-

date. But after 1957 the Cardinals were not sure he would do.

Fortunately a different Boyer showed up in 1958. Instead of sulking when criticized, he did his job cheerfully. He was finally left at third base and in each of the next four years he hit over .300. Musial stayed active for years longer than the Cardinals had expected. The Man kept swinging and the hits kept falling in. He remained King of the Cardinals. But Boyer soon became crown prince. In the early 1960's, Boyer was named team captain.

He developed a tremendous respect and liking for Musial in the nine years they played together. He sensed there was something Musial wanted very much—to play in one more World Series. The Cardinals hadn't won a pennant since 1946.

In 1963 the Cardinals were moping along in third place in August. They seemed to have little chance of catching the Dodgers. Then on a day off, club-owner Gussie Busch threw his annual picnic for the entire Cardinal team at his estate near St. Louis. It was a rainy day and the players and their families huddled inside Busch's mansion.

Then Stan Musial stood up and made an announcement. "I've made up my mind," the 42-year-old Man said. "I'm retiring after this season. I've played long enough. It's time to retire."

Boyer is a top third baseman. Here he leaps to catch a line drive.

When the Cardinals reported to Busch Stadium the next day, they had a cause. They wanted to win one last pennant for Musial. The Cardinals made their move. They won nine straight, then lost to the Mets. Then they won another ten straight games. Going into the middle of September, they were only one game behind the Dodgers. Then the Dodgers came to St. Louis for a three-game series. There was tremendous pressure on both sides, with huge crowds pulling for a Cardinal victory. But only Musial played good ball. The Man had four hits in three games. Boyer hit into thirteen straight outs and the Cardinals lost all three games. They were out of the race.

Boyer had his best season in the majors, driving in 111 runs. But his success was not very heartening: the Cardinals had lost the pennant.

After Musial's retirement Boyer's position as team captain meant more than it had in other years. "There is more pressure this year because Musial has left," Boyer said as the 1964 season began. "It's more an obligation to the younger players. They come to the older players for guidance. An older player can give them compliments, pats on the back and confidence."

Boyer also found time to think about himself. He suddenly realized that he was 33 years old and had never been in the World Series. "If you play for 12 to 15 years, I think it would leave you with an empty feeling not to have been in one," he said.

Ken knew all about World Series rings. Every fall his brother, Clete, returned to the family home in Alba, Missouri, with a new one. Clete was the third baseman for the New York Yankees.

It didn't look as if the Cardinals would earn their rings in 1964. Ken hurt his back diving for a ground ball in June. He batted only .227 that month and the Cards lost 17 of 28 games. They slipped into seventh place and Kenny heard the boos from the Cardinal fans.

"A player doesn't want to make excuses or alibis," he said. "A player doesn't want to take himself out of the line-up either. But my back really bothered me. The boos? They have the right to boo me. They have the right to expect a lot from a high-priced ballplayer."

Boyer felt better after the All-Star break. He hit .348 in July and the Cardinals won 17 of their 28 games. But owner Gussie Busch was impatient. He fired his general manager and almost fired manager Johnny Keane. Busch expected the Cards to finish halfway down the league. Then after the season he could fire Keane and hire somebody else.

Suddenly the Cardinals got hot. Boyer had batted

in 93 runs going into September. He knocked in nine more runs in the first eight games in September. When the Cardinals moved into Philadelphia they were only six games behind the league-leading Phillies.

In the first game the Phillies had a 5–4 lead going into the ninth. Relief pitcher Jack Baldschun got the first two outs. Then the Cards put two men on base, bringing up Ken Boyer. He slapped a single to center field to tie the score. The Cardinals won, 10–5, in the tenth.

Now the Cardinals had won 13 of 16 games. They were only five games out.

"I've got the feeling now that they might be peeking back at us a little," Boyer said. "After that hit I could tell by the look on their faces that they were demoralized and dejected. It's natural when you get a hit off their best relief pitcher."

The Phillies went into a dreadful September slump. The Cardinals moved up on them but the Reds moved faster. With one week left Cincinnati was in first place and the Phillies visited St. Louis for a three-game series. Once again Busch Stadium was packed with excited fans. The Cardinals were close to another pennant. The fans wanted to see them go all the way this time.

In the first game the Cardinals took a 1–0 lead

Boyer's bat kept the Cardinals alive late in the season.

after three innings. Then Boyer smashed a double
and went to third on Bill White's single. When
Julian Javier hit a ground ball to second base, Boyer
could have held at third. But he decided to try for
home. The throw came to catcher Clay Dalrymple,
who wheeled to make the tag. But Boyer had slid
across home with the Cards' second run.

In the fifth inning Boyer doubled again and scored

on White's single. The Cardinals won, 5–1, to move within one game of the Reds.

On the second night the Cards won, 4–2. On the third night Boyer had three hits and the Cards won, 8–5, to take over first place.

They held in first place over the final weekend and the season was over. The Cardinals were National League champions. Boyer had driven in 119 runs to lead the majors. He had a .295 batting average and 24 homers. Now he could play in his first World Series—against the Yankees and his brother, Clete.

The Yankees are always tough in the World Series. They won two of the first three games and lefty Al Downing was beating the Cards, 3–0, after five innings of the fourth game. The Cardinals had only one hit in five innings. The fans in chilly Yankee Stadium were rooting for a quick Yankee triumph.

Cardinals Carl Warwick and Curt Flood led off the sixth with singles. Then Yankee second baseman Bobby Richardson fumbled a ground ball, loading the bases. That brought up Ken Boyer. Downing pitched carefully. But Boyer found a fat pitch and slammed it into the left-field seats for a grand-slam homer. That gave the Cards a 4–3 lead and they held it for the rest of the game. Now the Series was all tied up.

After hitting his game-winning grand-slam home run in the 4th game of the World Series, Boyer is congratulated by the men who scored ahead of him.

The fifth game went into extra innings. White walked to open the Cardinals' tenth. Keane ordered Boyer, the clean-up hitter, to bunt. He placed a fine bunt near the pitcher's mound to move White to second. When the pitcher, Pete Mikkelsen, bobbled the ball, Boyer was safe at first. Seconds later Tim McCarver slugged a homer into the right-field seats.

The Cardinals had a 5–2 victory and they led three games to two.

The Yankees won the sixth game sending the Series into the deciding seventh game. The game was scoreless after three innings. Boyer led off the fourth with a single and the Cards scored three runs before the end of the inning. They scored three more in the fifth. Boyer doubled in the middle of the rally. The Cards led, 6–0. Then Mickey Mantle of the Yankees hit a three-run homer to make the score 6–3. In the seventh inning Boyer hit a homer to make the score 7–3.

The Cards needed every run they could get. Weary Bob Gibson allowed homers to Clete Boyer and Phil Linz in the ninth inning and the Cardinals just eked out a 7–5 victory to win the World Series.

Boyer's average for the Series was only .222. But he drove in six runs—all of them important. "This season couldn't have been any more satisfying," he said as his teammates congratulated each other in the clubhouse. "I think I did just about everything I had hoped to do."

In November Boyer was named the Most Valuable Player in the National League for 1964. "I don't know about deserving it," he said. "There are so many great players. Just say it's a great honor. That's the most important thing—the honor."

The next year wasn't nearly so good. He slipped to a .260 average with only 75 runs batted in and 13 homers. "A bad year," he said. "I don't know why." The Cards slipped with him. They finished in sixth place one year after being world champs.

Almost exactly a year after winning the Most Valuable Player award, Boyer was traded from the Cardinals to the New York Mets. At first he was very disappointed. He loved St. Louis and had made his home there. But then he realized that he still had some good years left in baseball.

"I'll put my whole heart and soul into the Mets, like I did for the Cardinals," Boyer said. He realized it wasn't easy to be a Most Valuable Player on a last-place team like the Mets. But he promised to do his best. Met fans knew that Boyer's best was very, very good.

14
ZOILO VERSALLES

Most Valuable Player, American League, 1965

I

It was a perfect afternoon in St. Petersburg, Florida, on April 5, 1965. The sun was shining down on the blue waters of Tampa Bay, just behind the ball park where the Minnesota Twins and New York Mets were playing an exhibition game.

But Zoilo Versalles, the regular shortstop of the Twins, was out behind the grandstand slouched against a tree. He was wearing brown slacks and a tan shirt, not a baseball uniform. He was drinking from a soda bottle. There were tears in his eyes.

168

He looked very carefully at the green bottle in his right hand. Then he fired it against the wall of the clubhouse. The bottle exploded against the brick and slivers of glass fell into the grass.

Why was Versalles so unhappy? He had just been taken out of the game by manager Sam Mele. There had been an argument between Mele and Versalles, and Zoilo knew he was in trouble.

The trouble had begun in the fifth inning. Versalles was playing shortstop and the Mets had runners on second and third. Jim Hickman of the Mets hit a ground ball to the left of Versalles. Versalles moved toward it but never touched it. The grounder went into center field for a single and two runs scored.

The runners had hardly touched home plate when the Twins' manager stood up in the dugout. A big strong man wearing the number 14 on his back, Mele waved at Versalles. He seemed to be saying, "Get yourself off that field this second. You didn't even try to stop that ball." Mele knew that Versalles could have stopped the grounder even if he couldn't have thrown the man out at first base. If he had stopped it, only one run would have scored. The Twins had finished in seventh place the previous year because of sloppiness and Mele wouldn't stand for it any more.

Versalles just stared at Mele. He couldn't believe that the manager would take him out of the game in the middle of an inning, with both teams and 2,000 fans watching. But Mele waved again and called to him. There was no doubt: Versalles was out of the game. A substitute shortstop was already running onto the field.

Versalles stumbled off the field. It took him a long time to reach the dugout. When he reached it, he took off his glove and slammed it down on the bench. Mele saw that.

"Sit on the bench," Mele said. "Maybe you'll learn something."

"I'll sit on the bench for Martin, not for you," Versalles snapped.

It was exactly the wrong thing to say to Mele. The newspapers had been saying that he was going to be fired if the Twins didn't make a good start in 1965. According to the writers the new manager would be Billy Martin, the third-base coach who had been added to the staff to put "fire" into the Twins, particularly Versalles. But instead of putting fire into Versalles, Martin seemed to be putting fire into Mele.

Mele was a gentle man who believed in treating his players as adults. He hardly ever raised his voice. But now he was shouting at Versalles.

"That will cost you a hundred dollars," Mele roared.

"Why not make it two?" Versalles snapped back angrily.

"I will," Mele replied.

"What about three?" Versalles continued.

"That's what it is," Mele concluded. "Now go in and take a shower."

Versalles didn't back down. He grabbed his glove and stormed off to the clubhouse. Once he had taken a shower, Versalles lost his anger. He realized he had defied his manager and would have to answer to the clubowner that night. He pulled on his street clothes, bought a soda and leaned against a tree behind the grandstand. That's when he smashed the bottle into a million pieces.

"I don't want to say anything about it now," Versalles told questioning reporters. "I don't want to talk until I see Mr. Griffith (the owner of the Twins) tonight. I'm going to tell him I want a little respect around here."

When the game ended, the other Twins showered and dressed. Then they all hopped on the team bus for the two-hour trip to Orlando, Florida, where the Twins make their spring-training headquarters. Versalles was a pathetic sight as the bus pulled away. He stared out the window, wondering what would happen when he got home.

Things happened fast that night. Mele gave Griffith his side of the story. He said that as long as he was manager, Versalles would have to pay the $300 fine. Then they called Versalles in.

They told him that the $300 would be taken out of his first pay check. They told him it was time for him to show what he could do. He was 25 years old and had been in the major leagues for four full seasons. At times he had done well but he didn't seem to try hard enough.

Versalles did not like to be told about his faults. In the past he had covered up criticism by bragging. "I think I am better than Luis Aparicio," he said when he was a rookie. "Zorro can make all the plays Aparicio can. Why he big hero and Zorro a nobody?"

The Twins had nicknamed him "Zorro" after the television character. It was easier for them to pronounce than his real name, which sounds like "Sol-yow."

The Twins didn't understand Versalles when he first joined the team in 1959. They didn't know that he bragged to cover up his fear. He annoyed them by complaining of an "aching back" whenever he made an error. But his back never hurt when he played well. His teammates called Versalles a "hot dog," which is a baseball term for "showoff."

In 1961 he left the team for three weeks and threatened to quit baseball. Calvin Griffith brought Versalles' wife up from Cuba to make him happy. He rejoined the team and Griffith did not fine him.

"What good would that do?" Griffith asked. Griffith knew that Versalles had been a poor boy from the slums of Havana, Cuba. He had gone without many meals when he was a boy. Money was valuable to him. Griffith didn't want to break his spirit by taking money away.

But that was in 1961. Now it was 1965. Versalles was four years older. He was supposed to behave better. He was also supposed to play better. Griffith told Versalles that he could be the best shortstop in the American League. He was small (only five foot 10 inches tall and 160 pounds) but he was strong and fast. He had good hands for a shortstop and his arm was strong. The only thing holding Versalles back was himself.

So the $300 fine had to be paid, and Versalles was on trial. Griffith and Mele warned him that 1965 was a make-or-break season for all of them.

The season opened on April 12 with floods surging all over the Upper Midwest. Metropolitan Stadium was drenched for Opening Day. But the game with the Yankees went on anyway. Zoilo didn't make a hit

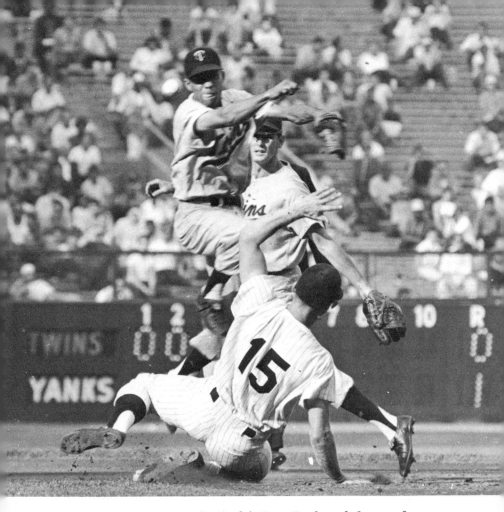

Versalles jumps over the Yanks' Tom Tresh and fires to first to complete the double play.

but the Twins beat the Yankees 6–5, in the eleventh inning. The season had begun on a winning note.

People soon noticed that the Twins were a different club. Instead of standing around waiting for one of their sluggers to hit a home run, as they had done in the past, the Twins slapped singles, stole bases and worked the hit-and-run.

"Go for the extra base," Mele urged them. "Take the chance. If you're out, I'll take the blame."

The Twins tried it and it worked. They raced to a 7½-game lead by August 10. But people still expected the Yankees to make a rally and overtake the Twins. That's what made the three-game series in Yankee Stadium so important. There were 29,529 Yankee fans watching the first game, waiting for the Twins to collapse.

Versalles led off the first inning with a ground ball to shortstop. In the past Versalles had loafed when he thought he had hit an easy out. This year he was hustling on every grounder. When Phil Linz bobbled the ball momentarily, Versalles was safe on the error.

Versalles was thinking hard as he reached first base. He knew that Yankee left fielder Mickey Mantle was slowed by leg and shoulder injuries. Versalles decided to take an extra base if the ball were hit to Mantle.

The next batter, Rich Rollins, slapped a hit to left field. Mantle hobbled for the ball and Versalles and Rollins tore around the bases. The Yankees had a choice: they could try to get Rollins at second base or Versalles at home. They elected to try home. But Versalles slid in safely and Rollins scooted into second. The Twins led, 1–0.

The next batter, Tony Oliva, slashed a single and Rollins scored easily from second. So the Twins had a 2–0 lead because Versalles had hustled.

The game wasn't going to be easy, however. The Yankees came back to tie the score, 2–2, going into the eighth inning. It was the time when Yankee fans could expect a typical Yankee rally.

Versalle batted in the eighth inning with nobody on and one out. He lined a single to center field. At least it should have been only a single.

"This is the kind of game where you have to take that chance," Versalles said. "When I step on first, I take a look. I see the ball six feet in front of Tresh. I knew the grass is high in the outfield. I keep running."

He saw that the center fielder, Tom Tresh, would have to rush the ball, which was slowed down by the high grass. So Versalles slid into second with a double before Tresh could return the ball.

"That was the big play," Yankee manager Johnny Keane sighed.

Rollins then hit a ground ball back to the pitcher. If Versalles had stayed on first, it would have been an easy double play. Instead Rollins was out at first and Versalles moved to third.

The Yankees still could have gotten out of the

Zorro bedeviled the Yankees all season. Here he scores on an inside-the-park home run.

inning without giving up a run. But this just wasn't the Yankees' year. They chose to walk Oliva on purpose and pitch to Bob Allison. It was good strategy because Allison tapped a grounder right back to the pitcher. But the pitcher, Pete Mikkelsen, heaved the ball right past the first baseman. Versalles scored to break the tie. The Twins went on to score five runs in the inning and win the game, 7–3.

The Twins lost the second game but won the third game. Versalles made seven hits in the three games.

In fact he murdered the Yankee pitching all during 1965. It was not an easy thing to do. The best players in the league have traditionally crumbled against the Yankees in important games. Versalles batted .342 against the Yankees, scored 24 runs, drove in 10 runs, stole four bases and hit four homers. He played better against the Yankees than he did against the rest of the league. And the Twins beat the Yankees 13 times in 18 games.

The Twins walked away with the pennant after that series with the Yankees. They won by seven games over Chicago; the Yankees finished 25 games out. Versalles batted .273 and led his club in runs, doubles and stolen bases.

"Zorro was our motor," said Billy Martin, who was still the coach.

"He inspired us to a pennant," said Sam Mele, who was still the manager. "His play in the field, his work at bat and his leadership led us to a pennant. There were others, but not as much as Versalles."

The Twins lost to the Dodgers in the seventh game of the World Series but Versalles batted .286 against the outstanding Dodger pitching.

And in November Versalles was named Most Valuable Player in the American League.

"I feel like a schoolteacher when one of her children graduates," said Billy Martin. "I'm very proud

Always a promising player, Versalles finally came through in 1965.

of Zoilo. He worked hard for it. He's a very intelligent player now. He used to be moody. Now he talks in the clubhouse meetings. He has an idea about making plays and where to play the hitters. I'm very proud of him."

"It is like a dream," Versalles said.

He was reminded of that day, six months earlier, when Sam Mele pulled him off the field in Florida.

"I don't get my money back but it makes no difference to me," Versalles said. "All season long Sam and I have been real good. We win the pennant, that's the big thing."

Somebody suggested to Versalles that the pennant and Most Valuable Player award were really won down in Florida, when Mele made Versalles grow up.

"Could be, could be," Versalles said.

The way his eyes twinkled, he meant "yes, yes."

INDEX

Page numbers in italics refer to photographs